The Inverse Engine:
Transforming Trauma into Purpose and Exponential Growth

By Greg E. Hollis

The Inverse Engine:
Transforming Trauma into Purpose
and Exponential Growth
By Greg E. Hollis
Alchemical Gold Publishing

The Inverse Engine: Transforming Trauma into Purpose and Exponential Growth

Publication Details

- **Publisher:** Alchemical Gold Publishing

- **ISBN (Paperback Print): 979-8-9945451-4-0**

- **Edition:** First Edition

- **Printed in:** USA

- **Cover & Interior Design:** Greg E. Hollis

- **Contact:** AlchemicalGoldPulblishing@gmail.com

D e d i c a t i o n

I dedicate this book to those who seek
to look beyond the surface in search of answers. May it
inspire and encourage those who need it most.

Acknowledgments

I'm grateful to all those I've met along the way - through friendships, work, patient care, casual connections, and fleeting encounters with strangers. Every interaction contributed to shaping the insights found in these pages. Without them, this book might never have come to be.

Figure I.1: **The Abyss** - A subtle fade into the unknown. The abyss isn't dark it's every color all at once.

Within us lies an energy, stronger than lightning,
lasting past mountains. When guided by intention,
it becomes an endless well of potential.

DEDICATION...4

ACKNOWLEDGMENTS...5

PREFACE..11

INTRODUCTION: 15

CHAPTER I: THE ENERGETIC RESONANCE EFFECT METHOD   19

CHAPTER II: THE MORTENSON SECRET: ACTIVATING YOUR A.M.E.   29

CHAPTER III: INDELIBLE: THE SHAME IMPRINT OF TRAUMA   39

CHAPTER IV: THE INVERSE ENGINE: TRANSFORMING TRAUMA   45

CHAPTER V: RESONANCE ARCHIVE: YOUR FIVE ENERGETIC
POTENTIALS 53

CHAPTER VI: THE OBLIQUE ANGLE: THE CUSTOM BLUEPRINT   61

CHAPTER VII: THE CHARGED LOOM: SELF-HONOR AND ENERGETIC
BOUNDARIES.......................................77

CHAPTER VIII: THE SILENT EBB: CLEARING ENERGETIC SLOP 87

CHAPTER IX: ECHOES OF FUTURE: RECLAIMING IMAGINATION WITH
THETA WAVE.......................................91

CHAPTER X: PULSE OF THE UNSEEN: MEDITATION FOR ENERGETIC
STABILITY 97

CHAPTER XI: THE FEAR-FORGED FLOW: TRANSFORMING RESISTANCE
INTO PURPOSE 101

CHAPTER XII: THE ABYSS COMPASS: BREAKING LIMITING BELIEFS   105

CHAPTER XIII: THE STILL POINT CURRENT: FOUNDATIONAL HABITS
FOR INNER PEACE 113

CHAPTER XIV: THE RIPPLE'S VOICE: LANGUAGE, PRESENCE, AND ENERGETIC INFLUENCE 117

CHAPTER XV: THE IGNITION THRESHOLD: NEUROPLASTICITY AND NEURAL REPAIR 125

CHAPTER XVI: THE WHISPER IN THE WAVE: UNLOCKING THE ENHANCED FRISSON EFFECT 135

CHAPTER XVII: THE VARIABLES LAB: SHIFTING YOUR TRAJECTORY 139

CHAPTER XVIII: THE CRUCIBLE EDGE: THE FORGING FIRE OF RESILIENCE 145

CHAPTER XIX: THE PRISM THRESHOLD: ADVANCED ENERGETIC INFLUENCE 149

CHAPTER XX: THE UNBECOMING: ALCHEMICAL GOLD AND EXPONENTIAL EXPANSION 155

CHAPTER XXI: LANGUAGE OF THE MEASURED HEART: YOUR MOST POWERFUL GIFT 160

AFTERWORD: 168

ABOUT THE AUTHOR 169

ALPHABETICAL INDEX & DEFINITIONS: ..170

INTELLECTUAL INFLUENCES: 177

Preface

Figure II.1: The Allegory of the Conscious and the Concealed. The surface narrative (City and Mind) is fed by the hidden current.

Preface

Take a deep breath, you're about to embark on a magical journey.

What if there were a language capable of translating the truth of your inner self into a clear, compelling force for change? What if you could learn to perceive the unseen energies shaping your life, and use them to author a new reality?

My journey toward creating this language began in 2018. What started as a curious experiment soon evolved into something far more expansive. I realized I wasn't just learning; I was pioneering an entirely new discipline I call **Elevated Energetic Transformation**. This methodology centers on the unseen, internal forces, the energetic residue of the past, that continue to shape our present results. While traditional approaches (e.g., conventional talk therapy, cognitive-behavioral therapy) often focus on changing behavior or managing symptoms, this work reaches deeper, guiding transformation at the energetic level. This book you hold in your hands is a powerful tool for awakening that capacity within you. If you are ready to expand your understanding of how emotion, experience, and energy intertwine, you are holding the right book, and prepared to explore a new dimension of self-mastery.

From this foundational idea, the Elevated Energetic Transformation (E.E.T.) model was born, a name that distinguishes my unique approach within this emerging field. This proprietary, systematic, and accelerated methodology draws from years of research and lived experience. It provides a clear pathway for understanding and transforming energy in daily life, activating authentic and irreversible shifts across all domains of being.

This book serves as your companion in discovering your own voice within this transformative language. Throughout its pages, you'll find imagery, metaphors, anecdotes, poetry, inspirational quotes and personal stories woven together to bring each concept to life. These elements invite you not only to understand but to embody the language of energy and transformation.

This is more than a book, it is a guide to an original methodology and a call to a deeper kind of self-discovery. The core of this work lies in the E.E.T. model and the B.E.T.E.R.

Framework, introduced in Chapter I. Your commitment to engaging with these systems marks the first and most essential step toward lasting energetic freedom.

May these pages uplift your spirit and awaken your inner rise, so that together, we elevate our shared human experience.

Key concepts at a glance

Energetic Transformation (E.T.)	E.T. the base term for the conscious process of recognizing, defining, and regulating subtle energy states (mental, emotional, vibrational) to drive core personal change, underpins all advanced energetic practices. My proprietary creation, Elevated Energetic Transformation, refines this foundational transmutation to its pinnacle
Elevated Energetic Transformation (E.E.T.)	E.E.T. this proprietary methodology accelerates systematic change beyond basic energetic awareness. It specifically targets the source energetic frequency to trigger irreversible, authentic shifts across all domains of life. These shifts culminate in a state of sustained elevated being.
Energetic Resonance Effect (E.R.E.)	E.R.E. the intentional and gracious practice of cultivating a harmonious inner state that infuses the shared field with coherent, uplifting energy. Through this attuned presence, a subtle nonverbal resonance emerges, an exchange that transcends words and improves mutational connection.
Authentic Magnetic Essence (A.M.E.)	A.M.E. the transmutation of one's sensual energetic essence, converting it into magnetic attraction and creating a presence that draws others toward us inevitably and authentically. This process represents a subset of the Energetic Resonance Effect.
The B.E.T.E.R. Framework	A five-step method for activating the Energetic Resonance Effect. It provides a structured way to align thought, feeling, and energy and action to create transformative internal and external impact.

Introduction:

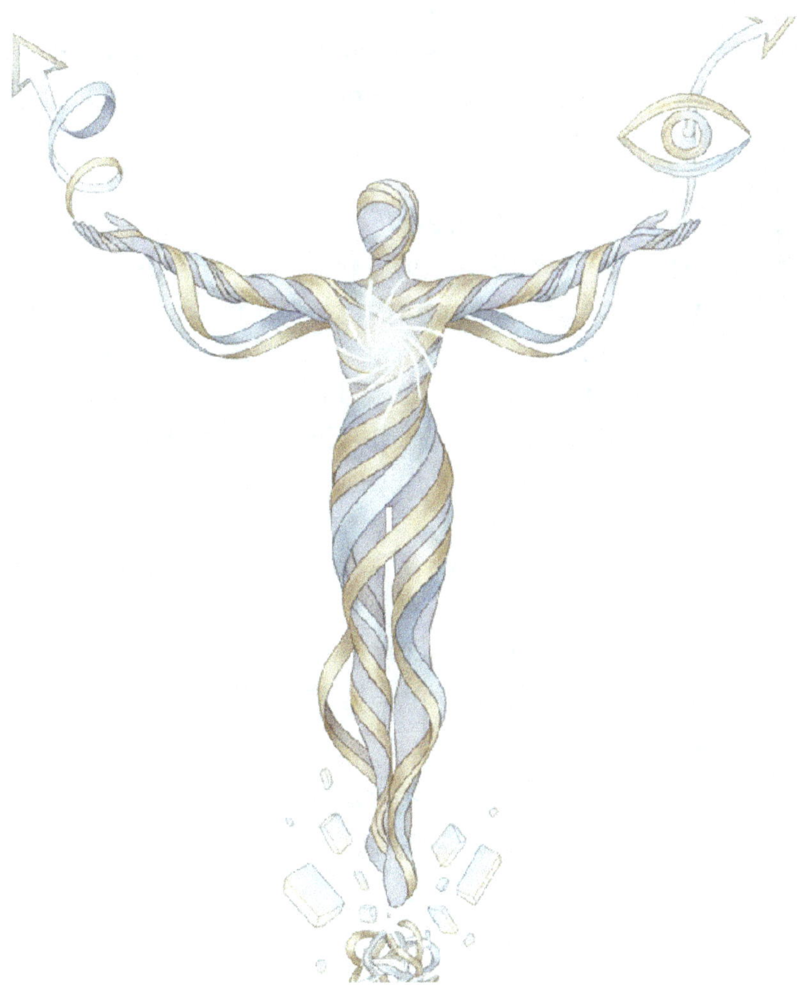

Figure III.1: Embrace the journey. This symbol embodies the fluid nature of energy and the empowered path of Elevated Energetic Transformation, guiding you to resonate with your truest self

Figure III.1: This image embodies Elevated Energetic Transformation (E.E.T.). A figure of golden and lavender ribbons stands with arms outstretched, radiating light from its core to signify conscious potential. An upward-spiraling arrow evokes growth; an eye with ascending arrow represents focused vision.

Introduction

Welcome to a new kind of self-help, one rooted in the pioneering field of energetic transformation. My approach, called **Elevated Energetic Transformation (E.E.T.),** is a groundbreaking method designed to help you reframe the way you understand and work with the energy in your life. At its essence, this process is about turning inward, learning to gather, focus, and shape your own energy as a force for conscious self-evolution.

This book is more than a collection of ideas; it is a practical handbook designed for tangible application. Together, we will explore the fluid and dynamic nature of energy, translating its power into a clear, structured process you can grasp and apply with confidence. You will be introduced to the proprietary B.E.T.E.R. Framework, a powerful structure designed to move you from stagnation to purposeful action, and from uncertainty to clear, focused intent. The full details of both the E.E.T. model and the B.E.T.E.R. Framework are waiting for you in Chapter I.

Prepare to embark on a journey that will awaken your inner potential and help you cultivate a life that feels truly authentic, one that mirrors your truest self. While the process is presented in practical terms, its construction is rooted in an unspoken artistic blueprint, providing a dimension of rhythm and form that guides the ultimate transformation.

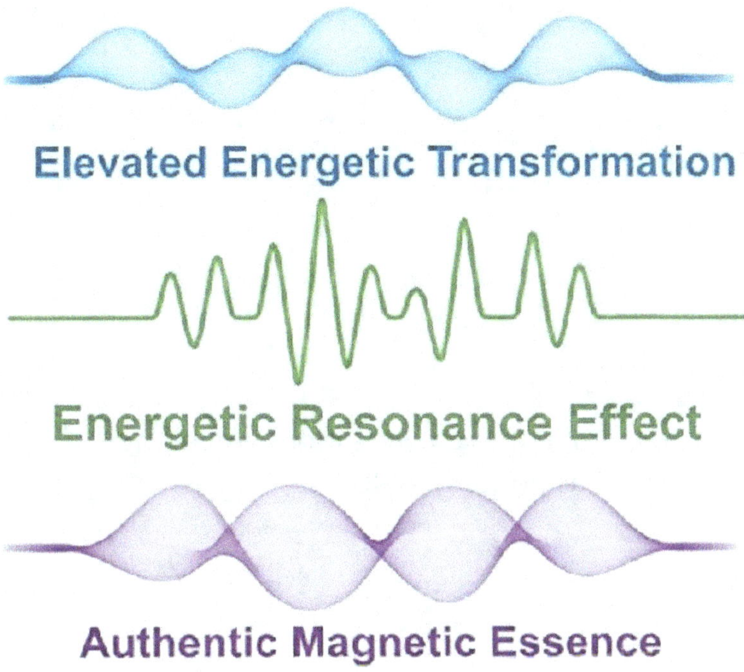

Figure III.2: The Three Pillars of Elevated Energetic Transformation E.E.T.

Figure III.2: Three waves illustrate the Energetic Elevated Transformation framework. Top blue wave (Elevated Energetic Transformation) flows softly like steady breath. Middle green wave (Energetic Resonance Effect) pulses sharply like a heartbeat. The bottom purple wave (Authentic Magnetic Essence) curves slowly for demonstrating true essence and harmony. Together they demonstrate interconnected frequencies.

There's an entire conversation happening
that has nothing to do with words…

Chapter I: The Energetic Resonance Effect Method

Figure 1.1: A visual representation of the **Energetic Resonance Effect.**

The Energetic Resonance Effect (E.R.E.):
A New Language of Connection

Have you ever noticed how some people seem to carry an invisible magnetism? They walk into a room and the energy shifts. They speak, and others lean in. What if this isn't just charisma or confidence, but a form of communication far more fundamental than words?

This book is built on a new idea: that a conversation can be happening that has nothing to do with words, it is the language of energy. It is the silent dialogue of presence, feeling, and intention.

At the heart of authentic connection lies the Energetic Resonance Effect (E.R.E), a form of wordless communication that transcends spoken language. This effect is grounded in what I refer to as the **Superimposition Principle**, which enables us to intentionally modulate our internal energetic state. Importantly, one cannot hold a negative mindset and create positive outcomes simultaneously; the higher frequency always dominates. By consciously elevating our vibrational energy to neutralize these lower frequencies, we gain direct control over our energetic output. This self-regulated state becomes what I call our Energetic Resonance Effect (E.R.E.), the unfiltered expression of our inner experience. When stabilized through the Superimposition Principle, the E.R.E. eases the burden of navigating complex emotional landscapes, allowing interaction to flow with clarity, harmony, and authenticity. In this state, communication becomes less about the words we choose and more about the energy we transmit, a subtle coherence that invites understanding without effort. The E.R.E. acts as a tuning mechanism, aligning inner intention with external expression so that what we project mirrors who we truly are.

The E.R.E. is the practical, outward expression of your energetic awareness, an intentional and gracious practice of cultivating a harmonious inner state that effortlessly infuses the shared field with coherent, uplifting energy. Through this attuned presence, a subtle, nonverbal resonance emerges, an exchange that transcends words and strengthens transmutational connections.

Each word you speak carries its own energetic frequency. When you infuse your language with conscious intention, you awaken a living exchange between expression and emotion, what I call an **Energetic Feedback Loop** where your internal state shifts first, and this inner coherence effortlessly shapes the energetic quality of every interaction. Through this process, awareness becomes embodiment, and understanding becomes lived experience.

To illustrate this, think of yourself as the conscious conductor of an orchestra. Your inner world is a symphony of a whole myriad of different sounds and energies. The E.R.E. serves as your baton, allowing you to direct a clear, unified melody, a higher, more affirmative vibration, that transforms any internal chaos into a cohesive and fluid symphony. The overall energy of your presence shifts from discord to harmony, creating a new, elevated state of being.

The shifts created by E.R.E. are not theoretical; they are experiential and immediate. Cultivating this purposeful energetic state establishes a new inner baseline that you can feel in every interaction.

These are the primary sensations and states that define the successful feeling of the Energetic Resonance Effect:
- Inner harmony flowing through your being.
- A rising strength that inspires clear, confidence.
- An angelic presence.
- Self-compassion that naturally uplifts self and others.
- A vitality that renews and brightens your spirit.
- Authenticity expressed with genuine integrity.
- A magnetic presence that draws others easily.
- A subtle, grounded confidence.
- An alluring, radiant state of existing.

Key Benefits of the E.R.E.
The E.R.E. unlocks a potent and healing state of being, cultivating the self-compassion needed to break free from old patterns and create a better future.

Mental and Emotional Transformation
The E.R.E. can be an empowering tool for healing past pain and trauma. At its core, this practice is based on a specific idea: you cannot simultaneously be stuck in negative thoughts and feelings and maintain an optimistic outlook. By actively fostering a more optimistic mindset, you can begin to retrain and shift your mind to favor an improved mental and emotional state, allowing you to move beyond past trauma. As I previously mentioned the **Superimposition Principle**

Physiological Benefits
Beyond these inner shifts, the Energetic Resonance Effect transforms not only how others perceive you but also how you perceive yourself. This heart-centered practice alchemizes negativity into optimism, expanding your personal energy while subtly uplifting the collective atmosphere around you. In this way, the E.R.E. serves as a conscious form of

shape-shifting, an inner vibrational shift that manifests as a distinctly different outer persona. Through cultivating stillness and quiet confidence, your energy begins to radiate with grace, depth, and effortless strength. Living in your optimal state is fundamental to this practice and offers significant health benefits. Practiced consistently, the E.R.E. becomes a powerful anti-aging ally, reducing the physiological impacts of stress and supporting the preservation of youthful energy, radiance, and overall resilience over time. This process is not a temporary fix but a transformative shift that becomes your new normal. You may find this state to be not only beneficial but also accessible and sustaining. As you begin this journey, even a small shift can initiate a cascade of meaningful change.

The influence of the Energetic Resonance Effect (E.R.E.) is not limited to interpersonal dynamics. This disciplined focus creates a powerful, elevated frequency that acts as a resource, sustaining and enhancing the practitioner's own state. This energy establishes a resonant field that spontaneously expands into the nearby space. Its stabilizing presence is palpable to any individual within range, contributing to a distinct restoration of life force in surrounding flora and fauna. Through this dedicated internal cultivation, the E.R.E. practitioner extends a transformative vibrational footprint that promotes healing and elevated well-being throughout their immediate landscape.

The Energetic Anchor Effect (E.A.E.)
This pervasive influence is what I call the **Energetic Anchor Effect (E.A.E.)**. Through the Energetic Resonance Equation (E.R.E.), the practitioner becomes the energetic anchor within their environment. You've likely noticed this effect in your own life: when you are present, the atmosphere of your home or workplace feels uplifted, things flow more smoothly, morale rises, and synergy unfolds naturally. Yet when you're away for an extended time, the space's inherent lower frequency can resurface, leading to a gradual decline in coherence or vitality. The E.A.E. illustrates that your conscious energy provides the sustaining frequency that holds any shared field in alignment.

The Energetic Operator
A "**transducer**", a term I use to describe those with this ability, is a person who perceives and interprets subtle energies and vibrations through the sense of feeling, experiencing intuitive impressions somatically via bodily sensations, emotional resonance, and energetic shifts. Unlike a seer, who receives insights visually, a **feeler** tunes into an embodied sensing of the unseen energies around and within people, places, and situations. This sensitivity guides heightened understanding, empathy, and awareness, serving as a powerful somatic complement to visual, visionary insight, and a foundation for energetic techniques anyone can cultivate. For enhanced accessibility, a **transducer** will also be referenced as a **'feeler'** throughout our discussions.

The ability of the **transducer** to sense and interpret subtle energies is the raw resource for transformation. However, raw sensitivity alone is not enough to generate consistent, reliable results; the power of the Energetic Resonance Effect is only fully realized through a structured, repeatable process. To this end, the B.E.T.E.R. Framework provides the systematic roadmap for the transducer to harness their inherent energetic sensitivity and intentionally transform trauma into exponential growth.

The B.E.T.E.R. Framework: Your Transformational Roadmap
The Energetic Resonance Effect (E.R.E.) emerges from a deliberate, five-stage process crystallized within the B.E.T.E.R. Framework, your foundational roadmap for conscious energetic transformation.

The Five Steps of the B.E.T.E.R. Framework:
1. **Be**: Ground yourself in the present moment.
2. **Elevate**: Choose a high-vibrational word.
3. **Transmute**: Transform the word into a felt emotion.
4. **Excite**: Amplify the feeling with an energetic charge.
5. **Radiate & Repeat**: Integrate the shift and repeat the cycle.

This framework is the engine of change you will learn to master. This is the first step toward becoming the conscious conductor of your life's symphony.

Reflective question:
What is one small energetic shift you could make today to feel more assured?

The Practical Guide: Activating the E.R.E.
The E.R.E. is a powerful phenomenon that enables you to consciously direct your energy to transform your internal state. This transmutational art, I like to refer to as: **Energetic Magic,** an innate ability we all possess. We will now delve into the specific techniques needed to activate and practice this effect, which can eventually become self-sustaining and automatic.

The B.E.T.E.R. Framework in Practice
Be: Grounding Your Baseline. This is your baseline. Before doing anything else, take a moment to settle yourself. Try this **60-Second Mindfulness Practice:** close your eyes and focus on the sensation of your breath for one minute. As thoughts arise, allow them to pass without engaging them. If your mind wanders, gradually guide your focus back to your breath without judgment. This practice helps release mental distractions such as

worry or overthinking, helping you feel more grounded and maintain a relaxed state necessary to cultivate this practice.

Elevate: (Setting Your Frequency). Elevate your state by choosing a high-vibrational word. Select one that resonates with you, such as self-compassion, optimism, or joy.

Transmute: Transmute the word into a feeling. Don't just think it, **feel it.** Recall a memory where you experienced that uplifting feeling and focus on the physical sensations associated with it.

Excite: Amplifying the effect. Awaken the feeling to give it energy. While holding that felt experience, infuse it with an energetic charge. This infusion activates and amplifies the word's inherent transformative power.

Radiate & Repeat: Integrate and radiate the felt shift. This convergence of feeling, excitement and transmutation activates the Energetic Resonance Effect. Continue to repeat this process from the beginning to sustain this elevated state and eventually it becomes automatic.

The B.E.T.E.R. framework is more than just a sequence of actions; it is a practical application of fundamental scientific principles, which we will now explore.

A Deeper Dive: The Science of Phase and Frequency
The Energetic Resonance Effect can be understood through the physics of **PHASE** and **FREQUENCY**, fundamental elements underlying all existence.

Just as radio signals require both the correct frequency and phase for clear reception, energetic connections between people require these same elements. Your thoughts and feelings generate energetic waves. Frequency refers to the quality of the wave (for example, joy has a higher frequency than sadness), while phase is the alignment between your thought and your feeling. When your thought about joy matches and aligns with the felt experience of joy, your energy becomes more coherent, more potent and more powerful!

B.E.T.E.R. Framework: Applying Phase and Frequency Principles:
- **Be**: Sets your baseline energetic state.
- **Elevate:** Sets your intended frequency (the energetic quality you're broadcasting).
- **Transmute**: Creates **Phase Coherence** (the alignment between mental intention and felt experience).
- **Excite**: Strengthens both frequency clarity and phase stability.

• **Radiate & Repeat**: Integrates the synchronized energetic field you've created.

This progression maps visually as:
Presence → Elevating Word → Transmutation → Feeling → Excitement → Energetic Resonance Effect → Radiate & Repeat the cycle.

The Power of Felt Experience

This process isn't just about what we think; it's about what we feel. The true power lies in attaching feeling to thought, transmuting a mental concept into an embodied experience. A felt experience matters more than going through life's routines. The ability to change our reality lies not solely in our thoughts but in the combination of thoughts and the sensations they generate. When we anchor our thoughts in sensation, we give them tangible quality and energetic density, creating a direct path for manifestation in the physical world.

The Result

The Energetic Resonance Effect emerges from these synchronized actions. Its benefits compound over time, creating an accelerating cycle of Elevated Energetic Transformation. To nurture this expansion, we must avoid internal disruptions such as worry, negativity, or self-sabotaging mindsets that could weaken or slow our process.

Through consistent practice, the E.R.E. becomes a self-reinforcing cycle, what I call an **Energetic Feedback Loop**. This strengthens the effect until it becomes an automatic, effortless state which I call **Energetic Autopilot**.

By pairing uplifting feelings with excited energy, we initiate a transformation process that eventually becomes self sustaining. This systematic application of the Energetic Resonance Effect significantly contributes to your overall journey within the Elevated Energetic Transformation process. As you consistently apply these techniques, your mind retrains to recognize possibilities once overlooked, equipping you with practical tools to navigate discouragement and or disappointment more effectively, preventing these moments from pulling you into negative mindset traps.

Reflective question

How is the feeling of this thought changing my experience right now?

~Transmute your energy, shape the reality you desire.

Chapter Summary: The chapter describes the Elevated Energetic Transformation (E.E.T.) framework, which is a practical way to use Energetic Resonance Effect to create change within your internal state and attract more of what you want. This process is summarized by **the Superimposition Principle and the** B.E.T.E.R. Framework, a five-step method for activating this effect. The method works by aligning the frequency (the quality of your energy) and phase (the alignment of your thoughts and feelings). Consistent practice creates an Energetic Feedback Loop that eventually leads to an automatic state called Energetic Autopilot, which helps you navigate life and avoid negative mindset traps.

Figure 1.3: The inner workings of the **Energetic Resonance Effect.**

Figure 1.3: By using the Energetic Resonance Effect to shift internal states and attract desired outcomes which aligns FREQUENCY (the quality of your energy) and PHASE (the alignment of your thoughts and feelings).

As you reflect on the Energetic Resonance Effect method and its possibilities, let the following poem serve as a reminder of the steady, radiant process unfolding within you. May it inspire you to nurture your energetic elevation with patience and joy, knowing that each small shift contributes to lasting internal changes.

The Radiant Shift

Be, in quiet presence, where the worries cease,

A starting point to find a healing peace.

Be in this moment, grounded and aware,

Release the thoughts that pull you here and there.

Elevate, with a word or feeling, bright and

bold, Imagine a future braver than the one once

told. Elevate your state and choose your inner light,

Let joy or purpose gently ignite your might.

Transmute the word, let feeling rise from deep,

A promise that your inner self can hold and keep.

Transmute with memory, recall a perfect day,

Feel warmth and ease that washes fear away.

Excite that feeling with a pulse of will,

A vibrant hum to make your spirit thrill.

Excite the energy, clear and strong and true,

A steady current flowing out from you.

Radiate the wave, the change you've made within,

Receive this new reality you can now begin.

Radiate the cycle, steady, strong, and sure,

Repeat, a self-sustaining flow that will endure.

Chapter II: The Mortenson Secret: Activating Your A.M.E.

Figure 2.1: **Energetic Magic** (aka **Energetic Transmutation**): This chapter, focuses on the transmutation (the transformation of thought into felt experience) and in turn the creation and enhancement of our Authentic Magnetic Essence (A.M.E.).

The Inner Current's Gaze

Within your light, a quiet threshold waits,

A clear perspective that now dominates.

No fleeting glance, nor shadow's passing art,

But sight that sees beyond the hidden part.

I watch the shape your inward self controls,

The unread chapter in your book of souls.

A subtle current stirs within your core,

A living truth you can contain no more.

For in the hush, beyond the words you speak,

A higher knowing both our spirits seek.

A quickened sense where wisdom takes to

flight, I see beyond the boundaries of light.

This inner witness, constant, clear, and true,

Awakens every light that shines in you.

A sudden knowing, luminous and fast,

A silent recognition made to last.

The Mortenson Secret: Activating Your A.M.E.

While researching energy concepts, I encountered a captivating social media account that described an elderly relative. The post highlighted the grandmother's unique and powerful presence, which the author referred to as having a "**Marilyn Monroe Effect**." This quality was described as a striking form of internal energy that seemed to transform the atmosphere of any room she entered, creating an irresistible attraction.

This particular description resonated immediately with my own experiences and observations. It perfectly encapsulated the transformative magnetism I had been working on and cultivating for years. Through numerous posts and discussions shared by different people across various platforms.

I eventually understood there was a concise, recognizable term already in our vocabulary for the specific energetic practice I was employing and that word is: **transmutation.**

Transmutation, in personal growth, is about creating change at your very core, moving beyond surface habits to transform your inner foundation. It's more than rearranging what others see; it's a journey of truly becoming someone new from the inside out. This powerful shift happens when you alter your energetic state, translating thought into authentic feeling. Just as true transformation changes the heart of matter, personal transmutation is a powerful change that renews your identity from within.

For years, I searched for how to describe what I was practicing; suddenly, the term was now obvious to me. Studying these concepts further, I realized this power wasn't reserved for Hollywood icons but was within reach for everyone, just waiting to be ignited.

Marilyn's Demonstration

Marilyn Monroe, born Norma Jeane Mortenson, possessed a remarkable quality that she would occasionally reveal. In my research on Monroe, I encountered an anecdote shared by Amy Greene, the wife of Monroe's photographer and a close friend, who recalled an afternoon when Monroe chose to demonstrate this unique ability.

"I'll never forget the day Marilyn and I were walking around New York City, just having a stroll on a nice day. She loved New York City because no one bothered her there like they did in Hollywood, she could put on her plain Jane clothes and no one would notice her. She loved that. So as we we're walking down Broadway, she turns to me and says 'Do you want to see me become her?' I didn't know what she meant but I just said 'Yes'-

and then I saw it. I don't know how to explain what she did because it was so very subtle, but she turned something on within herself that was almost like magic. And suddenly cars were slowing and people were turning their heads and stopping to stare. They were recognizing that this was Marilyn Monroe as if she pulled off a mask or something, even though a second ago nobody noticed her. I had never seen anything like it before."

— Amy Greene, wife of Marilyn Monroe's personal photographer, Milton Greene.

Figure 2.2: A visual representation of the **Magnetic Essence** within.

Figure 2.2: A trench coat, worn by an unseen presence, stands open to reveal a luminous ethereal silhouette radiating light and swirling energy from its core, transforming an ordinary exterior into a captivating **Magnetic Essence** within.

This moment exemplifies the power of energetic mastery: Monroe's skill arose from a rare discernment, a refined self-awareness and finesse that allowed her to shift her presence from an unassuming passerby to a magnetic figure at will and in an instant. Though celebrated for her beauty, her deeper strength lay in this ability to transform, an intentional redirection that instantly altered how she was perceived. By activating and amplifying her inner vitality, she could embody magnetism at will. This transformation occurs when sensual energy is transmuted into a more potent personal signal, what I call **Authentic Magnetic Essence (A.M.E.).**

Key Concept: Authentic Magnetic Essence (A.M.E.)
Authentic Magnetic Essence is the transmutation of embodied sensual energy into magnetic presence, cultivating an authenticity that effortlessly draws others in. This process operates as a subset of the Energetic Resonance Effect.

Two Expressions of Transmutation
Elevated Energetic Transformation manifests in two primary forms: **the Energetic Resonance Effect and Authentic Magnetic Essence.** These complementary tools shape how we connect with others. The E.R.E. focuses on infusing language with intention, recognizing that words carry energetic resonance that shapes how they're received. When our inner state aligns with outward expression, both the message and its impact are transformed.

In contrast, Authentic Magnetic Essence isn't rooted in speech but in how we channel essential vitality. It's the art of transmuting sensual essence into a refined personal signal, one others can easily sense even before we speak a single word.

Think of your A.M.E. not as an always-on feature but as a frequency you learn to transmit intentionally. Like a starship engaging its cloaking device to travel unseen, you can modulate your A.M.E. to remain inconspicuous when needed. Monroe's ability to shift from invisible to magnetic demonstrates this mastery, the deliberate toggling of presence from subtle to radiant. To deepen the practice, consider how alignment and intention work together. These following key definitions clarify how congruence and modulation interact:

Energetic Congruence is a state of alignment where actions, words, and decisions reflect your inner energy, your E.R.E. In this state, your energy transmits a unified signal, enabling the A.M.E. to broadcast effortlessly.

Energetic Incongruence is a misalignment that arises when actions stem from doubt, fear, or patterns that dilute your authentic current. This weakens your signal and disrupts the natural flow of A.M.E, reducing your energetic impact.

Operating in Energetic Congruence

Functioning from energetic congruence allows your outer world to mirror the clarity of your A.M.E. Each purposeful act reinforces your unique energetic signature, dissolving resistance and transforming every task into a fluid expression of your authentic self.

Intentional Energy Direction

Once congruence is established, the next step is conscious direction. Rather than dimming your essence to fit external patterns, refine and focus it with deliberate awareness. This is the art of what I call **Focused Energy Shaping,** embodying the frequency you intentionally choose to project. It is not about performance, but a return to your core. You attune inward to the pure resonance of your A.M.E., allowing that current to effortlessly shape every interaction.

As your inner alignment strengthens, the E.R.E. rises. Others respond not to a superficial image, but to the resonance of your authentic state. You no longer adjust to the room's energy; instead, you elevate it through your own. This coherence bridges the biological and subtle realms: your primal essence flows through both hormonal balance and refined energetic resonance. While hormonal responses arise instinctively, your energy can be consciously guided, transforming reactive impulses into radiant, intentional presence.

Activating Authentic Magnetic Essence (A.M.E.)

Authentic Magnetic Essence activates when its raw current is consciously recognized, refined, and expressed. Awareness comes first, acknowledging the reservoir within. Through focus, this energy can be amplified, shaped, and transmitted through conscious communication. As vitality merges with refinement, it becomes an unmistakable signature of presence. This essence remains fluid, never fixed. At times it expresses guardedness; at others, openness or playfulness. A.M.E. shifts effortlessly with circumstance, expanding or contracting according to how freely we allow it to move through us. People often sense this current before they fully perceive and comprehend it. Words may mask, but energy never lies. By observing how our essence radiates, we learn to refine its expression. Intentional embodiment arises from inner discernment, ensuring that what we project remains an expression of integrity, not imitation. Through awareness and deliberate direction, what was once unconscious becomes radiant, magnetic, and quietly transformative.

The Mortenson Secret

That day on Broadway, Monroe was doing more than displaying charm, she was demonstrating energetic command. In an instant, she shifted from an ordinary passerby to a magnetic presence, not through costume or performance, but through the transmutation and focus of her own internal essence.

The insight she embodied was unmistakable: true allure is never surface-deep. It arises from the deliberate transformation of one's inner energetic current. This understanding captures the foundation of **Authentic Magnetic Essence** and marks the path of this journey.
The grandmother who could illuminate every room lived by the same principle. Her "Marilyn Monroe Effect" was no act, it had become an effortless extension of her being. That same capacity rests within each of us, waiting to reawaken.

Reflective question: How would you describe the qualities of the essence you currently project?

~ We attract more of what we desire when we react less to what we don't.

Chapter Summary: This chapter describes a person expressing what's been referred to as the Marilyn Monroe Effect, paired with an anecdote from Monroe's friend Amy Greene. Monroe's ability to become magnetic at will reveals that true power comes from consciously shifting inner energy, not appearance. The concept of Authentic Magnetic Essence (A.M.E.) is introduced as the art of transforming sensual vitality into radiant presence that shapes how others perceive us. Two expressions of transmutation are explored: the Energetic Resonance Effect, which infuses words with intention, and A.M.E., which refines authentic sensual energy into a subtle personal signal felt before words are spoken. Focused Energy Shaping is also introduced as the practice of refining hormonal capacity. The chapter's core message: magnetic presence lives within everyone and can be awakened through awareness and intentional focus to amplify authenticity and expand personal energy.

This poem captures the dramatic, powerful moment of energetic command, the deliberate shift from being unseen to embracing a fully magnetic presence.

The Unveiling

A simple coat, a silent street,

A fleeting glance from passing feet.

A hush descends, a whisper streams,

To stir the veiled, to part the seams.

No word is spoken, no name is known,

Yet something other makes itself shown.

The current bends, the air now clears,

A hidden fire through shadow peers.

Not face, nor dress, nor crafted art,

But quiet truth that floods the heart.

The secret breathes, the tether breaks,

A presence takes, an **essence wakes**.

Figure 2.3: A visual representation of **Authentic Magnetic Essence** activated.

~ Those struggles you've endured happened for a reason. They made you stronger, more resilient, and shaped your character. Don't quit now.

Chapter III: Indelible: The Shame Imprint of Trauma

Figure 3.1: Indelible - A visual representation of early struggles and their lasting imprint.

Figure 3.1: Indelible: A solitary child curls in a dark fetal position, surrounded by thorny vines labeled 'FAILURE,' 'DIFFERENT,' 'UNWORTHY,' and 'DESPAIR.' Fragmented memories scatter across a cold, isolated landscape, with a faint, distant whisper of hope threading through the darkness.

A Childhood of Misunderstanding

My journey didn't begin in theory, it began in the raw terrain of painful childhood experiences. These were more than memories; they etched a lasting, low-vibrational imprint on my sense of self. I remember silently crying as my father tried to explain a math assignment, his efforts faltering while my frustration turned inward. What was wrong with me? Tears blurred the page, and his disappointment thickened the air. Though he never met my eyes, I felt his frustration, my shame and hopelessness intensified. The assignment remained unfinished, and with it, my last threads of hope became unraveled. From those quiet, tear-streaked moments, I learned a painful truth: asking for help often invited more pain. So I withdrew. That inner tightening marked the emergence of a wounded Energetic Resonance Effect, a pattern I would one day learn to transform.

When the familiar discouragement continued to repeat with my teachers, the growing weight of academic pressure and relentless self-criticism soon triggered a wave of OCD traits. These manifested as obsessive counting and a fixation on even and odd numbers, avoiding cracks in sidewalks and tiles, flicking lights on and off in ritualistic patterns, untangling every fringe on rugs, and struggling with facial tics. I never understood why I was compelled to these rituals, but they seemed to offer a sense of safety in a world that often felt unstable. Ashamed and confused, I became exceptionally skilled at concealing these habits, so adept that even my family, classmates, and friends rarely noticed.

I remember the sting when classmates handed back my tests, their eyes fixed on my failing grades. Tears blurred the red marks as I escaped to my cubby, pretending to search my coat pockets, hiding my face. What should have been playful, innocent years were shadowed by humiliation and quiet despair. Each morning, dread grew as I approached the school bus. School became a landscape of isolation. In the cafeteria, I ate alone, invisible. Gym class brought new shame, being picked last for teams, and unwanted. Even recess offered no relief; I stood at the edges of the playground in the tree's, hearing laughter that never included me.

Beyond social barriers, I frequently stayed after school, struggling to keep pace. Summers slipped by in remedial programs, always trying to catch up while others played freely. Eventually, the weight of it all led to my being held back in third grade, severing the few friendships I'd managed to form and deepening my isolation among unfamiliar faces.

Eventually, through testing, my struggle was given a name: "learning disability", a term now softened to "learning difference". The diagnosis explained my challenges but also deepened a sense of brokenness. My parents' attempts to clarify only widened the gap I felt from others. This was my first encounter with what is now called "neurodivergence", a way of thinking outside the mainstream. Classroom rules and social cues remained mysterious, leaving me without a map. In special classes, surrounded by a couple other so-called misfits, my anxiety, depression, sense of aloneness, and hypersensitivity only seemed to grew stronger.

For much of my life, I moved through a world that felt subtly out of sync, though I didn't yet have the language to explain why. I now understand that what I once called "Internal Weather" was often the result of auditory processing delays, a literal lag in how my brain translated sound into meaning, along with dyscalculia, which created a persistent friction with the numerical world.

These weren't deficits in the engine but distinct calibration settings. Recognizing these neurodivergent traits allowed me to stop viewing my mind as broken and begin seeing it as a unique processor, one that simply requires its own kind of fuel.
Everything came to a head in high school. Years of isolation, academic struggles, and the persistent belief that I was fundamentally flawed had accumulated into a weight almost too heavy to bear. The anxiety and depression that had lingered since childhood deepened into frequent episodes of very deep depression. As my shame turned inward, the low-vibrational imprint of those early years took its most perilous form: thoughts of suicide began to surface frequently. Eventually, those thoughts led to action, I tried to cope by cutting my wrist. I still remember the uncomfortable, panicked moment when a fellow student, and then my science teacher, noticed the scars. Fear surged through me as I worried they might report me, exposing my hidden pain in the classroom. Those silent acts were a desperate response to ongoing suffering. Even so, I maintained a facade of normalcy, masking this crisis behind a practiced exterior, pretending everything was okay. I carried this weight of confusion and diminished confidence into adulthood

When Failure Becomes Identity
My neurodivergence has fundamentally shaped my identity, leaving an indelible mark. The negative self-perceptions from school lingered, while the labels and judgments I absorbed from others gradually eroded my self-worth, shaping both my self-image and expectations for the future. These beliefs made me hesitant to seek help, especially since earlier attempts had only increased my confusion. The social distance I felt made close friendships and meaningful connections more difficult, intensifying my isolation.

Growing up neurodivergent in predominantly neurotypical environments, spaces designed by and for 'standard' brains, forced me into constant self-questioning. These experiences laid the groundwork for my adult relationships, embedding deep self-doubt and leaving childhood wounds unresolved.

As a result, I doubted I was worthy of care or appreciation, especially if I couldn't appreciate myself. The principles of Elevated Energetic Transformation later revealed a way to revise this inner blueprint, to finally feel deserving of connection. I learned early to make myself invisible, avoiding interaction and mastering the art of disappearing. What began as protection eventually hardened into habit, becoming my default way of navigating the world. The outcome was a strong sense of isolation that restricted my growth and prolonged my healing beyond trauma.

The Science Behind the Imprint
Complex Childhood Trauma (C.C.T.) is insidious. It doesn't just wound in the moment, it rewires a child's internal blueprint of identity and connection. Neuroscience explains why these patterns persist into adulthood. The developing brain, especially vulnerable to shame, lacks the fully developed prefrontal cortex necessary for emotional regulation. By ages two and three, children begin comparing themselves to social standards but can't yet separate their actions from their inherent worth. This developmental gap transforms every failure into perceived proof of personal flaw rather than a simple misstep.

Research by Mills et al. (2016) shows that this process, spanning childhood to adulthood, fundamentally shapes self-concept. When a child repeatedly experiences failure or trauma, deep shame takes root. The child learns to internalize blame, believing each hardship is their doing. This shame obstructs self-compassion and often endures into adulthood, manifesting as a relentless inner critic whispering, "I'm unlovable," "I'm a failure," "there's something very wrong with me."

Childhood shame ripples into adult relationships, undermining intimacy and trust. Early shame, research shows, can make secure bonding more difficult and strengthen patterns of approval-seeking, rejection anxiety, or emotional withdrawal. Later chapters will demonstrate how these shame-based imprints are precisely what the Energetic Resonance Effect can help release. Once rooted, shame shapes how we handle conflict, ask for support, and connect emotionally throughout our lives.

Looking back, I see how every classroom failure became evidence that I was fundamentally flawed. Misunderstandings and moments of alienation didn't fade, they solidified into beliefs about who I was and what I could become. That is the tragedy of childhood shame: it transforms temporary adversity into a seemingly permanent identity.

Reflective question:
How have the echoes of your past struggles shaped the person you are today? For instance, do you withdraw from social situations because of past isolation, or hesitate to ask for help after negative experiences?

Chapter Summary: This chapter explores how complex childhood trauma leaves a lasting imprint on the internal blueprint that shapes identity and relationships. Early struggles, including academic difficulties, social challenges, and a learning difference diagnosis, are shown to embed cycles of shame, inadequacy, and isolation. These early imprints persist into adulthood, fueling a harsh inner critic and obstructing secure attachments. Recognizing the enduring roots of shame is a vital insight that marks the first step toward transformation. This chapter invites readers to begin revising their own stories by reflecting on the shadows they carry from childhood alongside the light they seek.

A glimpse into the quiet struggle of invisible pain and the hope that lingers.

Shadow Against the Wall

Invisible, not by magic,

but beneath shame's weight,

I was a shadow pressed against the wall,

words frozen, lips silent,

retreating to the corners of despair,

where magic became hope,

wished for, never granted.

Tracing invisible lines

that lingered long past the bell,

alone at lunch, unheard,

heart pounding with terror

at whispered names.

Labels pressed like stones,

etched beneath skin,

where tears softened their edges,

and not belonging

became a quiet friend,

stitched of another thread,

soft, yet set apart.

But shadows cling to light,

and though weight bends the body,

it cannot break the thread,

a fragile flicker waits,

magic summoned from

the fragile thread of will,

pulling shadows into light.

Chapter IV: The Inverse Engine: Transforming Trauma

Figure 4.1: The Inverse Engine: Cultivate the intricate mechanics of your mind. A guide to nurturing your inner world and watching yourself thrive.

Figure 4.1: The Inverse Engine: An exploded view of golden gears and shafts, rearranged into a resilient mind forged by adversity, entwines symbiotically with vibrant green vines and leaves. The greenery channels past challenges into sustenance, growing through the intricate gears without impeding their smooth motion. A rounded wooden wheel and central radiant light emphasize its natural, powerful drive, turning trauma's energy into fuel for post-traumatic growth and an empowered, integrated identity.

The Inverse Engine: Transforming Trauma into Growth

I realized that while I understood the "what" of my childhood trauma, I was still missing the "how", the crucial, subconscious process that often fueled both my stagnation and my drive.

The missing piece of the puzzle came from an unlikely source: an online post by a fellow acupuncturist I had never met, Dr. Andrew Miles, L.Ac. The moment I read his words, I felt a striking clarity. His observation about suffering was more than a clinical insight; it was a powerful truth that illuminated the perspective I had held for so many years. He wrote:

"If you want to *destroy* someone, or even an entire group of people, just convince them that their suffering is special, that no one else has suffered in the same way they have. Because as soon as people start to believe that their suffering is uniquely special, they lose their capacity for compassion, their ability to connect with others, and their ability to heal." — Dr. Andrew Miles, L.Ac.

Recognizing Your Blind Spots

Reading that quote brought a powerful insight. I realized I had unknowingly fallen into what I call the **Uniqueness Trap** the unconscious belief that our suffering is somehow different from everyone else's. This belief closes the heart, blocks compassion and connection, and ultimately limits our capacity to heal.

For much of my life, I carried the belief that my childhood pain was worse than that of others. It created a sense of separation, making it harder to connect, heal, and see myself as worthy of love. That insight revealed how viewing my struggles as uniquely severe had kept me trapped in isolation and stagnation, unable to experience the shared humanity that allows growth and belonging.

Recognizing our personal blind spots is among the most important acts of introspection we can undertake. With awareness comes clarity, of who we are, where our weaknesses lie, and what drives our behavior. The moment we see these patterns clearly, they begin to lose their power over us.

This pivotal recognition, that my perceived unique suffering was a self-imposed block, allowed me to explore a corresponding truth: the hidden power and relentless drive that the wound itself had unexpectedly created.

Before continuing this journey, this poem reflects the quiet yet steady ignition that arises from struggle, the source of resilience and motivation that guides us toward transformation. Consider it a glimpse into the inverse engine that drives achievement, shaped not by ease, but by challenge.

The Spark

From shadowed childhood, silent fires start,

A hidden spark that fuels the restless heart.

Not born of drive, but shaped by pain's design,

A blueprint carved where love was hard to find.

In brokenness, a fierce strength will rise,

A quiet power behind aching eyes.

The vines of growth entwine the golden gear,

Transmuting pain to light, from doubt to clarity.

"If I achieve, I will be seen," it sings,

A drive born deep of trauma's stinging wings.

The engine turns with light that softly grows,

From pain to power, the true self shows.

Cultivate the intricate mechanics of your mind.

The Blueprint of High Performance

While navigating the complexities of my neurodivergence, I uncovered a key truth: the source of my resilience. Sometimes, the missing piece of the puzzle comes from an unexpected place, like a voice halfway across the world. This is exactly what happened when I encountered an interview with retired CIA officer, Andrew Bustamante. Speaking on his podcast, The Everyday Spy, Bustamante shared how the agency approached identifying high-potential candidates. I found his perspective to be a powerful anecdotal touchpoint that resonated with my own energetic findings, particularly his discussion on the surprising link between early life challenges and the drive for success. Below is a quote that describes his insights into this phenomenon:

"The CIA understood what to look for in a candidate before they became successful. And that magic element, that secret sauce that so few people realize, is that high performance is closely tied to childhood trauma. There is empirical evidence showing this; there are studies out there that show it. There is an actual chemical change in your brain during your formative childhood years that makes you essentially addicted to seeking approval and validation. If you don't have childhood trauma, you don't have that chemical addiction. So, if your parents love you, and everybody's there for you, and life is easy, you'll find yourself thinking, 'I don't need to prove myself, I don't need to make anybody happy.' But when you don't have that, when Dad doesn't pay attention to you because he's addicted to work, that is a predictable, trainable element within your psyche."
— Andrew Bustamante, The Everyday Spy Podcast.

In another interview, Bustamante expanded on this idea, explaining that:
"One of the first lessons you get at the CIA, at least in field operations, is that there is a strong, empirical connection between childhood trauma and high achievement. The science is out there; I've looked it up on my own. The connection is extraordinary: people who experience the right amount of childhood trauma, enough that you had to prove something, but not so much that you had to adopt external coping mechanisms, are turned into high achievers. This isn't because they were born with drive. It's because some part of their childhood, during those formative years, taught them that achieving will lead to a reward. That becomes the inherent thought: 'By achieving, I will be rewarded."
— Andrew Bustamante, The Everyday Spy Podcast.

Bustamante's analysis revealed that high performance is closely connected to childhood trauma. Empirical studies reveal that trauma during formative years can trigger chemical changes in the brain. Not everyone is affected in the same way; those who grew up in consistently loving, secure environments often lack the internal drive to feel compelled to constantly prove themselves because they don't feel a need to seek external validation. The "right amount" of trauma is key. Bustamante explains that too much trauma can lead to maladaptive coping mechanisms, such as substance abuse or emotional instability. However, just enough trauma can create a psychological blueprint where achievement is subconsciously equated with emotional reward. This cycle becomes foundational, driving individuals throughout life with an ingrained belief: "If I achieve, I will be rewarded." The energetic residues of trauma can be transmuted, not just healed. This concept is supported by research into Post-Traumatic Growth Inventory (PTGI), pioneered by

Tedeschi and Calhoun, which suggests that suffering can lead to significant positive psychological change and higher function.

The Post Traumatic Growth Inventory (PTGI)
In exploring research related to Bustamante's observations, I came across the concept of **Post-Traumatic Growth Inventory (PTGI)**. This phenomenon describes the positive psychological changes that a person can experience as a result of a traumatic life event. While Bustamante's remarks did not cite this framework, the themes he discussed, the potential for positive change following adversity, resonate with and mirror the core principles of the PTGI. To understand and measure this growth, I turned to a seminal work by psychologists Richard G. Tedeschi and Lawrence G. Calhoun: the Post-Traumatic Growth Inventory (PTGI). Published in 1996, the PTGI is a psychological assessment tool designed to measure these positive outcomes across five key domains:

- **Personal Strength:** An enhanced sense of personal resilience and capability.
- **New Possibilities:** The recognition of new opportunities and life directions.
- **Relating to Others:** Improved interpersonal relationships and social connections.
- **Spiritual Change:** A deepened spiritual understanding and religious growth.
- **Appreciation of Life:** Greater gratitude and appreciation for everyday experiences.

This research underscores how adversity can be a catalyst for resilience, adaptability, and personal growth, which are all highly valued qualities in demanding fields like intelligence work.

The Connection Between PTGI and Transmutation
As I explored this framework, I began to see my early experiences in a new light. The adversity I faced during my school years shaped how I processed challenges, and over time, I found myself using transmutation to navigate the complexities of adulthood. Although the research behind the Post-Traumatic Growth Inventory (PTGI) does not explicitly reference adults using transmutation as a conscious tool, I began to see a clear parallel. The PTGI suggests that childhood adversity can foster reward-seeking behaviors that extend into adulthood, laying the groundwork for transmutation as a coping and growth strategy. It offered me a new lens for understanding how early hardship can prepare an individual for transformation, especially when facing difficult life transitions.

To illustrate how these concepts manifest in lived experience, I examined the story of Marilyn Monroe, whose life powerfully reflects Post-Traumatic Growth. Monroe experienced significant early adversity: her father was absent, and her mother was institutionalized, which led to years spent in orphanages and foster homes. These environments exposed her to instability, neglect, and trauma. Beyond these external circumstances, Monroe also faced internal challenges, as she had dyslexia and a stutter, both of which fall under the umbrella of neurodivergence. Yet despite it all, she exhibited remarkable emotional resilience.

She underwent a form of post-traumatic growth that emerged as transmutation, a survival and success strategy. Her ability to channel personal hardship into greater magnetism became a defining feature of her public and private life. Monroe's past, marked by instability and trauma, acted as a powerful inverse engine. She transmuted her breakdowns into the very fuel for her breakthroughs, using pain as the catalyst for creativity, achievement, and self-reinvention.

The connection between my journey and Monroe's becomes clearer through the lens of Post-Traumatic Growth Inventory. We both faced early adversity that instilled a drive to equate achievement with validation. While the PTGI explains the "what," transmutation illuminates the "how." It is the conscious act of taking the original blueprint, the drive born from trauma, and purposefully redirecting it. Monroe did not grow passively; she actively transmuted pain into the magnetic strength of her persona. This process reveals that PTGI is not merely a byproduct of trauma but an intentional, adult method for shaping one's destiny and identity.

Conclusion: The acknowledgment of a Sacred Wound, the realization that personal pain is not unique but is isolating, is the first critical step toward channeling the raw, subconscious drive it created. Drawing from former CIA officer Andrew Bustamante's insights, we see how trauma during formative years can create a psychological blueprint where achievement is subconsciously linked to emotional reward. This understanding introduces the concept of Post-Traumatic Growth Inventory (PTGI) the positive changes that arise from difficult experiences, and shows how we can consciously choose to transform pain into personal power, much like Marilyn Monroe did with her own challenging past. The inverse engine concept, symbolized by her journey, proves that a personal breakdown can be the fuel for a breakthrough.

The Audacious Embodiment: From Critic to Catalyst

The journey begins when you claim your place as your own unwavering authority, unmoved by the consensus of the crowd. Shed the urge to label and let go of the inner resistance that feeds judgment. The path ahead calls for a decisive mental shift, one that transforms belief into full embodiment, replacing doubt with a consciously chosen, audacious story of self. Through this transformation, you become a radiant source of potential, a living catalyst dissolving the mental barriers of all who encounter your authentic presence.

Reflective Question: In what ways might your own past challenges have created a subconscious drive toward achievement, and how can you begin to consciously transmute that drive into a deliberate source of empowerment?

The following poem captures the essence of the journey from pain to purpose, an embodiment of the 'Inverse Engine' that fuels transformation from within.

The Inverse Engine

Fractured gears beneath the skin,

Whispers echoing deep within.

Vines of emerald weave and climb,

Breathing life through rusted time.

From distant lips, a truth takes flight,

A cipher carved from silent night.

Not frailty, but a wellspring's call,

Built on promises, standing tall.

Through tangled growth, my spirit weaves,

Strength woven through shattered leaves.

Each fractured gear a glowing mark,

Sparking flames to pierce the dark.

Silence speaks in subtle hues,

A summons bright to light anew.

From trauma's crucible, I rise,

Transmutation in my eyes.

Chapter V: Resonance Archive: Your Five Energetic Potentials

Figure 5.1:: Where Fire and Water converge in vaporous release, transmuting chaos into the radiant **Prismatic Core** of high-vibration consciousness.

The subtle, wordless truth of your core energy speaks first. Let this poem reflect that unspoken introduction.

The Unsaid

The surface holds its practiced line,

Yet something hums beneath the shine.

A glance, a breath, a fleeting beat,

I catch the trace of your retreat.

No walls can hide what energy may,

The truth emerges, soft as day.

No need for keys or stated plea,

What you intend is clear to me.

Your Invisible Introduction

Before you ever speak a word, you're already communicating. Each of us radiates a unique energetic frequency, what I call our **Core Energetic Signature**, which is the frequency an individual projects, maintains, and inevitably gravitates toward emitting. This constant energetic broadcast serves as an invisible introduction to everyone we encounter, often forming powerful first impressions in mere milliseconds. Improving our Core Energetic Signature is where the powerful Energetic Resonance Effect comes in as a very effective tool.

Think about it: when you walk into a room, people immediately pick up on whether you're projecting low, mid, or high vibrational energy. While they'll notice your appearance, hear your voice, and observe your demeanor, that initial energetic reading happens first and colors everything that follows. Your cells collectively generate this distinctive vibrational pattern that precedes you into every interaction. The exciting part? Once you understand the Energetic Resonance Effect principles, you can intentionally shift this energy to influence how others perceive and respond to you. By practicing Energetic Resonance, you gain the power to modify your vibrational signature and transform the way people experience your presence, all before uttering a single word.

Reflective question: What is your Core Energetic Signature... and what is one small thing you could do today to intentionally shift that energy?

Your Extraordinary Energetic Potentials

What if you understood you have a toolkit of powerful, innate abilities that could help you intentionally shift your energetic signature? In this chapter, we'll explore what I call our most **Extraordinary Energetic Potentials**: **Transmutation**, **Optimism**, **Imagination**, **Resilience**, and **Authenticity**. These are not external forces you need to acquire, but abilities already within you. Cultivating these five potentials is the primary mechanism through which you consciously shape, raise, or refine this Core Energetic Frequency. By becoming more consciously aware of them, you can unlock their transformative power and use them to shape your daily life.

Extraordinary Energetic Potential: Transmutation
Transmutation is the art of transforming one substance, form, or state into another. In this book, it refers to the process through which thoughts crystallize into feelings, the essential method for creating change at the level of identity. It is the act of becoming the architect of your emotional experience, transforming who you are at your core.

This power awakens not through logic or reason, but through feeling. You cannot think your way into this energetic shift; it must be sensed, felt, and lived.

The more you engage in this conversion, the more seamlessly it flows. The process is so innate that few can clearly describe how it works. No one ever taught us this ability, yet we've been practicing it effortlessly since birth. Try explaining it to a robot, the subtle, intuitive nature of it reveals just how strongly human and instinctive it is.

Many overlook this potent inner mechanism, taking it for granted. Yet when consciously used, it can elevate your state of being, helping you transform your circumstances and move beyond lingering emotional pain. Through transmutation, thoughts become feelings, and from those feelings, new realities are born.

Transmutation is the vital capacity that activates and refines the other four Extraordinary Energetic Potentials, turning them from abstract ideas into lived experiences. With this understanding, we can now turn to one of these four Extraordinary Energetic Potentials, Optimism, one of the more powerful energies available to us.

Extraordinary Energetic Potential: Optimism
Optimism is a powerful form of energetic openness, inviting the possibilities that exist in any given moment. Its energy serves as an organic companion to both transmutation and the Energetic Resonance Effect, acting as a catalyst within our energetic practice. Rather than displacing negative outlooks, the transmutation of optimism refines and elevates its vibrational frequency, deepening its effect. Transmuting optimism improves not only our disposition but our entire mode of being in the moment. When we consciously transmit optimistic energy, we effortlessly become more magnetic to those around us, encouraging a similar state of being in others.

The Foundation of Perspective

Our outlook has a strong influence over how our world unfolds for us. Like a master architect who understands that the foundation determines the strength of the entire structure, our fundamental perspective shapes and influences many aspects of our lived experience. When we operate from a negative outlook, we inadvertently construct a limiting experience. This pessimistic architecture constrains our vision, narrows our options, and brings forth our most fearful and defensive responses. Conversely, when we approach life with an optimistic outlook, we tap into much higher potential energetic and expand our possibilities. This foundation allows us to see opportunities where we might have otherwise seen obstacles, solutions where others may have seen problems, and growth where we may have experienced setbacks.

Optimism opens the doorway, and **imagination** steps through it.

Extraordinary Energetic Potential: Imagination

Imagination serves as our gateway to possibility, the fundamental capacity that allows us to envision and shape our preferred reality. Through imagination, we design desired outcomes before they manifest. This mental faculty gives birth to creativity, which then transforms our visions into tangible results. The transmutation of imagination is what elevates this process, as it refines the raw potential of a mental vision into a more focused and powerful energetic blueprint.

Consider the world around us: every human creation, from the simplest tool to the most complex technology, began as someone's imaginative vision. Buildings, art, innovations, and solutions all emerged from the ability to see beyond current circumstances and envision something new.

~ Our brilliance knows no bounds, limited only by the reach of our imagination.

Of course, not every day will be perfect. When we face challenges, we can use our ability to transmute **resilience**, turning adversity into strength.

Extraordinary Energetic Potential: Resilience

Resilience is the strong internal power that we can tap into to navigate difficulties and, more importantly, to emerge stronger from them. Whenever I have faced what once seemed like an insurmountable challenge and moved through it successfully, I have discovered that transformation was indeed possible. The transmutation of resilience enables us to convert the raw energy of adversity into refined strength and wisdom. What once appeared overwhelming often becomes the catalyst for unexpected growth and self-discovery.

Each time we persevere through hardship, we expand our capacity for growth and deepen our understanding of what we are truly capable of achieving. This process builds upon itself, reinforcing our resilience, which strengthens our sense of self-worth, bolsters our confidence, and enhances our ability to face future difficulties with grace and determination. The more we cultivate resilience, the more readily it becomes available, allowing us to see challenges not as obstacles but as opportunities for meaningful growth and development. Ultimately, our ability to transmute all of these potentials leads to our most powerful state of being: authenticity.

This union of softness and strength mirrors the path toward **authenticity,** the final and most essential energetic potential.

Extraordinary Energetic Potential: Authenticity
When we aren't living in our true authenticity, we may unconsciously create a false persona. Our authentic integrity, the truest and most potent part of our personality, when denied, creates a disconnect that others often easily sense. To compensate, we might incessantly seek validation or conform to external expectations, which only strengthens the divide between the self we present and who we truly are. This false persona emits a hollow energy that lacks genuine personality. The transmutation of authenticity strengthens our genuine core, allowing us to radiate a more powerful and true energetic signal. With in-authentic energy, we cannot ignite our Energetic Resonance Effect and remain disconnected from our true selves. Personally, I've noticed that when I allow my authentic self to come forward, it stirs an extremely potent and at times intoxicating energy inside me. It's hard to put into words, but it creates a blissful feeling that helps my self-compassion expand and dissipate any inner criticism.

Authenticity and Transmuting Thrive Together
When we cultivate a regular practice of transmuting authentic energy in our daily lives, we inherently encourage our true nature to emerge and expand. This interplay is not a flat or linear progression; rather, it acts as a vigorous unfolding of the self that builds in intensity over time. Consequently, this process feels intoxicating because it triggers a radical release of buried emotions and energy patterns. As these charged blockages that once obscured our expression dissolve, they leave behind a state of neutrality and wholeness. Since it is impossible to be inauthentic while transmuting pure authentic energy, these two elements authenticity and transmutation share a dynamic connection. They rely on each other to coexist in their most powerful state, culminating in a stronger sense of self.

The Feather and the Beast

Energy does not always roar. Sometimes it is a whisper.

Soft as a feather's brush, a ripple across still water.

Other times it surges, an unshackled beast reshaping all it touches.

We hold them both within us:

the feather and the beast-

one soft as morning light,

the other fierce as the coming storm.

Some days we are all feather,

drifting easily through quiet hours.

Other days the beast awakens, hungry,

demanding what was long denied,

shattering chains we never knew we bore.

But on rare, sacred days,

they rise as one:

the beast with a feather's grace,

fierce power clothed in tenderness,

a strength that bends without breaking,

a wildness that chooses its purr.

In their union, change arrives like rain-

hard enough to cleanse,

soft enough to let life take root.

Reflective question:
Do you routinely allow yourself to exist in your most authentic potential state? If not, why not?

Chapter Summary: This chapter revealed that your Core Energetic Signature is the unseen energy and message you project out to the world, shaping every interaction before words are ever spoken. It forms the basis of the Energetic Resonance Effect, which can be consciously refined. The five Extraordinary Energetic Potentials, Transmutation, Optimism, Imagination, Resilience, and Authenticity, serve as the inner tools that shape this signature. Energetic Transmutation converts our thoughts into felt experience, activating the others. Optimism expands possibility, Imagination designs new realities, Resilience turns adversity into growth, and Authenticity ignites our presence. Together, these potentials raise your core frequency so your silent message resonates with power and truth.

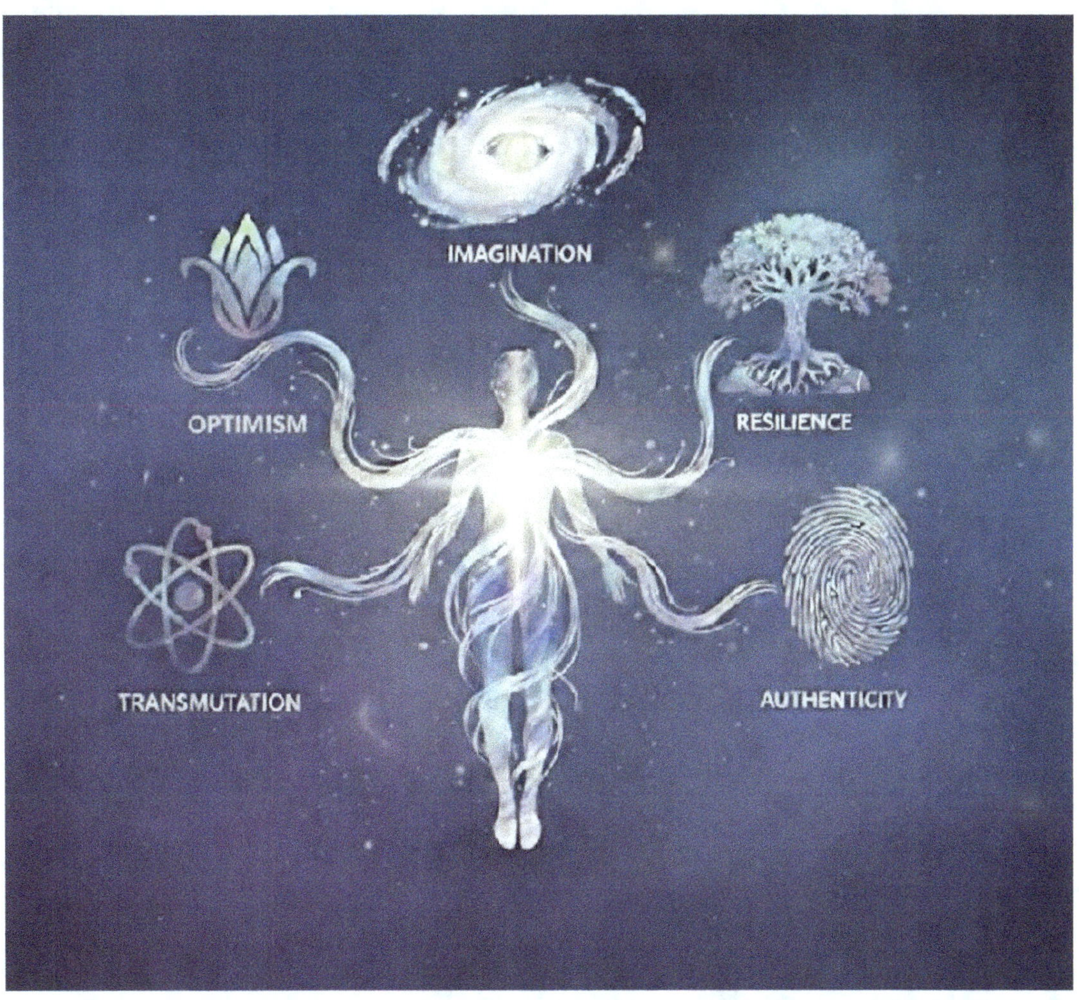

Figure 5.2: Visualizing the **Five Extraordinary Energetic Potentials.**

Figure 5.2: A luminous, translucent figure stands at the center, radiating five interconnected energetic abilities: **OPTIMISM** (lotus flower), **TRANSMUTATION** (atom), **IMAGINATION** (swirling galaxy/eye), **RESILIENCE** (rooted tree), and **AUTHENTICITY** (fingerprint spiral) the image embodies inner strength and consciousness flowing outward to shape experience and potential.

To close this exploration, let's return to where it all begins, your energetic introduction to the world. Long before you introduce yourself, the world has already received your message…

Core Signature: The Invisible Signal

Before a single word is spoken,

Your energy sings, unbroken,

A silent song, your core's own tune,

Shaping every glance, each room.

Your cells hum out a hidden beat,

Radiating essence, subtle, sweet,

Before your voice or face is shown,

A truth within, quietly known.

Within you rests a quiet power,

Transmuting thought in every hour,

Lifting lotus petals high,

Imagining vast, open sky.

Rooted deep in strength and grace,

Shining bright through time and space,

This beacon gleams with every breath,

Guiding how the world sees depth.

So ask yourself, in silence deep,

What melody does your spirit keep?

And how will your song begin today,

To shape the world in your own way?

Chapter VI: The Oblique Angle: The Custom Blueprint

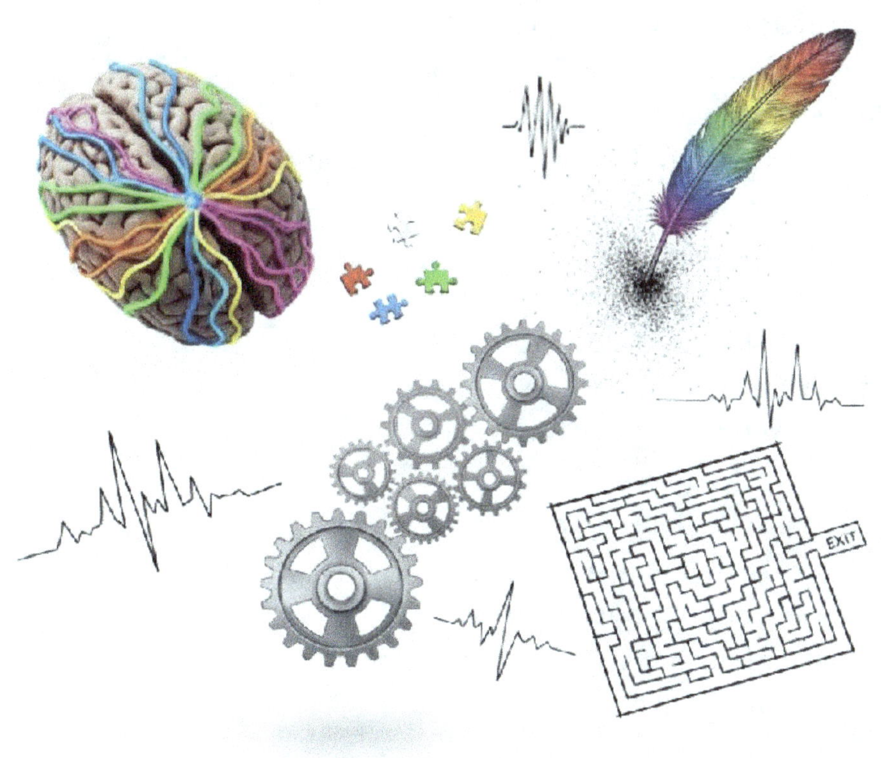

Figure 6.1: Navigating a complex **NEURODIVERGENCE**: A journey through creativity, challenges, and understanding.

Figure 6.1: A stylized, multi-colored brain with fiber optic-like tendrils represents unique **NEURODIVERGENT** wiring, connecting to misaligned gears that symbolize diverse cognitive processing. Fragmented puzzle pieces and erratic frequency lines depict a non-uniform cognitive rhythm. A convoluted maze with an exit sign shows challenges navigating a neurotypical world, while a rainbow feather quill symbolizes the creative strengths and unique expression emerging from this cognition.

This reflection explores the complex reality of navigating a world that often fails to see the value in a different way of thinking.

Shades of a Broken Spectrum

In a world split black or white, left or right,
blind to the colors in between,
I was caught in a web of cause and effect.
From my first breath, a system wired me from the start.
Invisible signals slipped through my beginning,
promising safety, yet humming with decay.
The shadowed hand of care offered protection,
but its decree fractured me,
like charged light through silicon, etching mutations
into a bright, bewildered spectrum
that no one learned to read.
Power turned from nurture to interference,
its glow too constant, too close, too clear.
But in time, reflection softens the break.
Shards scatter, refracting new hues;
strategies stir from stillness,
and hope hums its quiet repair.
I begin to gather what was scattered,
painting peace from patterns of static,
a nervous system of signals, finally my own.
Now the spectrum grows whole again,
softly first, a steady pulse,
then rising, unbroken, radiant:
a signal no longer borrowed, but mine alone,
shining without apology,
born of fracture, now finer for it.
What sought to distort
has only charged me brighter than before.

The experience of operating on a different wavelength can feel isolating, yet this separation is where unique strength is forged. This poem explores that necessary friction.

Out of Phase Toll

A perfect wired cage contained the flow,

Where mirrored faces fed the constant glow.

They drank the light their shallow pool displayed,

A reflecting surface where no shadow strayed.

I saw the fault lines in the constant gloss,

My spirit hummed an **out-of-phase toll**.

I am the shadowed hue the others fear,

A heavy truth their brittle frame won't hear.

What they perceive as interference and friction

Is my deeper current breaking from their fiction.

A different depth, a quiet, growing stream,

The unspoken logic that defies their dream.

They stay tethered to the brittle root,

While I transmute the charge to precious fruit.

I am the spark that leaves their orbit wide,

The solitary gold the fire refined inside.

A Different Operating System

The mind is like an intricate image, an expansive landscape woven with countless connections and mechanisms. What appear as flaws or differences are, in truth, the unique pathways that allow neurodivergent individuals to navigate the world from an oblique angle. While a neurotypical mind often charts a direct, familiar course through challenges, the neurodivergent mind embarks on alternative routes, crafting distinctive and creative solutions along the way.

Thinking of neurodivergence as a different operating system for the brain helps bridge understanding. It operates on a different bandwidth, an expanded spectrum of perception where sensory data, emotion, and thought move at uncommon frequencies. In this field, ordinary input can feel amplified, and social cues that seem straightforward to neurotypical may arrive as distorted or delayed signals. Unique learning styles, attentional patterns, and processing speeds shape how neurodivergent people tune into the world, often requiring more deliberate decoding of what others treat as automatic.

The effort to navigate life without a clear map often brings increased anxiety, frustration, and isolation, as if constantly managing congestion on an overloaded channel. Yet within this different wiring lies strength. The need to continually monitor, reroute, and translate experience fosters an extraordinary cognitive skill: **metacognition**, the capacity to notice one's own thinking and consciously adjust how mental resources are allocated.

To truly appreciate this experience, it is vital to recognize how fundamentally different neurodivergent and neurotypical minds engage with the world's unwritten rules and shared "signal standards." This understanding not only opens pathways to empathy but also reveals the richness in diverse ways of sensing, processing, and being.

The Cognitive Cost: Why Neurodivergent High-Resolution Processing Caps the Workday

For years, I thought my short work window meant something was wrong with me. I could operate with strong focus and intensity for about four to five hours, but after that mark, my energy would drop off abruptly, and my cognitive reserves would become depleted. This sharp and predictable drop in energy felt like a flaw I had to hide. Later, I discovered it's actually a common experience among neurodivergent people, driven by the high energetic cost of our cognitive style. The neurodivergent brain often operates in a kind of high-resolution mode, absorbing and analyzing enormous amounts of sensory and contextual data at once. This can create periods of extraordinary focus and efficiency, but it also places intense demands on internal resources, depleting them much faster than in neurotypical processing. Once that energy threshold is reached, typically long before a standard workday ends, the brain enacts a protective slowdown to stave off exhaustion, and energy sharply declines. Ultimately, our ability to achieve remarkable depth and speed in a concentrated time is our strength, and recognizing our energy limit is what preserves that valuable high-output capacity.

Neurodivergent Approaches to Social Frameworks

Neurotypical's often display an innate inclination toward social and behavioral alignment, their minds readily absorb and adapt to unspoken expectations, stepwise routines, and societal scripts. This manifests as a fluid ease with following established systems and protocols. By contrast, neurodivergent individuals commonly navigate the world through a distinct lens, guided by internal logic, nuanced pattern recognition, or passionate interests rather than conventional social signals. Their engagement is less about inheriting ready-made templates and more about crafting personalized frameworks that may diverge from mainstream norms. This fundamental difference underscores a split in cognitive style: the first favors smooth adherence to collective systems, while the second seeks authenticity through unique, self-fashioned pathways.

A significant challenge in bridging understanding between neurotypical and neurodivergent ways of being lies in their differing priorities of focus. When interaction is guided by unstated and shifting social rules, the essential element is often lost. The result is this:

The __neurotypical__ mind becomes so absorbed in the leaves of custom that they often overlook the vital root system of human connection.

For the neurodivergent individual, the root system is the __only__ language that matters; the leaves are merely confusing, superfluous noise. This vital root system is woven from authenticity, energetic integrity, and mutual presence, the living network beneath outward custom where genuine connection takes root and transformation occurs. It is the subtle field in which meaningful exchange is felt, a domain far deeper than etiquette or habit. For those attuned to energetic realities, this rooting becomes the signal and source of true understanding. When presence flows into the root system, communication transcends words and gestures; energy becomes palpable, intention is sensed, and the boundaries between self and other momentarily dissolve. In this space, unseen but undeniably real, transformation begins, emerging from the shared ground where authentic essence is both given and received.

Social Punishment for Authenticity

Neurotypical people often feel uncomfortable around neurodivergent individuals because they notice their differences and resistance to conformity or groupthink. As a result, they may target, attack, triangulate, exclude, mock, gossip about, or harshly criticize them. This social punishment creates environments where neurodivergent people must choose between authenticity or acceptance.

Metacognition as a Strategy for Neurodivergent Minds

Metacognition is the awareness and understanding of one's own thought processes. Neurodivergent individuals often rely more heavily on this skill, in contrast to many neurotypical people who navigate social and cognitive demands through implicit processing. This reliance stems from the systemic mismatch between core cognitive styles, sensory experiences, and prevailing societal expectations. As a result, constant, deliberate self-reflection on thinking, planning, and self-monitoring becomes a necessary tool for navigating a world not always aligned with one's neurotype. This active self-awareness enables neurodivergent minds to break down complex tasks, explicitly analyze social cues that might not be grasped implicitly, and develop personalized coping and learning strategies. Consequently, frequent engagement with metacognition fosters a unique strength: enhanced resilience, greater capacity for independent learning, and powerful self-regulation for managing cognitive or sensory differences.

Prioritizing Equitable Justice for the Neurodivergent Community

Justice is critical for neurodivergent individuals because it ensures that their unique ways of thinking, communicating, and experiencing the world are respected and affirmed rather than judged or suppressed. Genuine justice recognizes that equality does not mean sameness, it requires creating systems and opportunities that actively facilitate diverse neurological experiences. When equity and understanding guide our approach, neurodivergent people can thrive in education, work, and community life without being forced to conform to norms that fail to honor who they truly are.

This perspective of justice goes beyond mere inclusion; it demands a cultural and systemic shift toward recognizing neurodivergent identity as valid and whole. It challenges deficit-based models and promotes autonomy, cognitive liberty, and self-determination, ensuring that neurodivergent people are not just included but empowered to define their own realities and environments. Justice for neurodivergent individuals is fundamental, not merely for fairness, but for their dignity, thriving, and full, authentic participation in society.

The Weight of Being Misunderstood

Navigating a world built for neurotypical cognition often leaves neurodivergent individuals in a near-constant state of being misunderstood. Their distinctive ways of processing information, communicating, and engaging with the environment, whether rooted in learning differences or other forms of neurodivergence, are too often misread not as diversity, but as defiance, incompetence, or flawed character. This gap between inner reality and outward perception forms a recurring pattern: sincere efforts to connect or contribute are met instead with confusion, dismissal, or even hostility. The continual invalidation and ensuing negative treatment, ranging from exclusion and lost opportunities to outright ostracism or punishment, can take a severe psychological toll, compelling many to expend immense energy masking their authentic selves to endure a society that penalizes deviation from its norms. Yet paradoxically, this very inclination toward authenticity often nurtures a deep, non-negotiable integrity and a heightened discernment, enabling neurodivergent individuals to quickly recognize and withdraw from environments or relationships that lack sincerity.

Understanding Neurodiversity: An Overview

Neurodivergence encompasses a wide range of neurological and developmental differences. This starts with Learning Differences or Learning Difficulties, which are varied processing styles like visual, kinesthetic/tactile, and auditory approaches. This category also covers conditions like ADHD (Attention-Deficit/Hyperactivity Disorder), dyslexia, dysgraphia, dyscalculia, and dyspraxia. The spectrum also includes Language and Communication Differences (such as Developmental Language Disorder), Autism Spectrum Disorder (ASD), Asperger's, and Sensory Processing Differences, where the nervous system over- or under-responds to stimuli. Additionally, neurodivergence can involve intellectual and developmental differences, neurological conditions like Tourette syndrome, stuttering and epilepsy, and mental health conditions such as schizophrenia and neurodevelopment components such as OCD (Obsessive Compulsive Disorder), anxiety, and mood disorders. This overview is not all-encompassing, as the range of neurodivergent conditions is diverse and continues to evolve with ongoing research and understanding.

The Friction of First Impressions: Neurodivergent Social Barriers
It's an unfortunate reality that neurodivergent individuals are often met with initial unease or even quiet resistance from neurotypical people, particularly in first encounters or the early stages of a relationship. This reaction arises not from any personal flaw, but from a fundamental mismatch in social operating systems. Neurodivergent communication styles, differences in eye contact, body language, tone, or conversational pacing, often diverge from the unstated social norms neurotypical people use to build comfort and rapport. These differences are easily misread: directness can seem rude, quietness detached, and passion overly intense. As a result, the neurodivergent person may be placed at a subtle distance before genuine understanding has a chance to form, left carrying the emotional weight of being misinterpreted from the very start.

Neurodivergent Challenges with Social Interactions
For many neurodivergent individuals, maintaining eye contact during conversation can be distracting and even trigger sensory overload. This occurs because neurodivergent brains often process more sensory and social information simultaneously than neurotypical brains do. In such moments, looking away is not a form of avoidance, it is a regulation strategy. Many neurodivergent "hear" and understand better when they are not forcing eye contact, as direct gaze can overwhelm the senses with an excess of visual and emotional data. Rather than fostering connection, it can disrupt focus.

Looking away or anchoring attention on another object is not a sign of rudeness or disinterest; it is a self-regulation tool that allows deeper engagement without sensory overload. By respecting this need, communication becomes more authentic and aligned with an individual's neurological wiring, rather than pressured by social norms. These dynamics shape many aspects of daily life and become especially pronounced in dating, where subtle emotional cues and reciprocity carry heightened importance.

Neurodivergent Challenges in Dating

Dating can pose unique challenges for neurodivergent persons, especially when navigating the unspoken social rules that shape romantic interactions. The subtle cues of flirtation, body language, tone shifts, and implied meanings, can feel like a foreign language without a clear guide. For instance, avoiding eye contact might be misread as disinterest, while communicating with straightforward honesty may be perceived as intensity. These tendencies aren't choices but reflections of distinct ways of processing and understanding information and expression, which also influence friendships and partnerships. What some interpret as rudeness, rigidity, or obsession often stems from genuine expression, focus, and a preference for clarity.

As a result, many neurodivergent individuals find themselves torn between masking their authentic selves to gain acceptance or staying genuine and risking rejection. In this light, solitude becomes less about retreat and more about integrity and self-preservation.

Challenges of Social Norms in Neurodivergent Communication

When navigating neurotypical social norms, communication can be challenging for neurodivergent individuals who favor direct, authentic expression. Their open and direct style can be perceived as jarring or unsuitable because it often clashes with the unwritten neurotypical rules of communication. As a result, their words may be scrutinized and misinterpreted as deviating from expected social rules. What one person experiences as unfiltered honesty, another may misunderstand or even criticize, which creates constant pressure to monitor language. This dynamic makes it difficult for neurodivergent people to communicate freely and authentically with neurotypicals.

Why Passive Aggression Is Especially Challenging for Neurodivergent Individuals

Passive aggression presents a distinct challenge for many neurodivergent individuals, whose communication style values directness, clarity and honesty. Indirect remarks, unspoken resentments, and hidden expectations place an undue burden on the listener (neurodivergent) to interpret meaning, an effort that is often draining and ineffective. Far from being a subtle way to handle conflict, passive aggression can feel overtly hostile and unnecessary. Neurodivergent people tend to prefer direct, transparent communication without ambiguity or hidden agendas, as it fosters genuine understanding. Instead of resolving issues, passive aggression often obscures the core problem and damages trust, leaving many neurodivergent wondering why others won't say what they mean.

Neurodivergent Experience of Gender Roles

For neurodivergent individuals, traditional gender roles can be experienced as external impositions rather than authentic expressions of identity. A neurodivergent person may perceive gender roles as performed roles or "costumes" rather than inherent truths and tend to critically question societal gender norms. This perspective fosters greater openness to diverse, fluid, and expansive gender identities, with the focus being on acting out of authenticity rather than conformity. Neurodivergent experiences of gender may be more internal and less centered on social validation or performative community belonging, reflecting a unique way of processing gender beyond typical social scripts of neurotypicals.

Hypersensitivity in Neurodivergent Individuals

Neurodivergent hypersensitivity involves an expanded sensory and emotional perception, where the nervous system processes stimuli more intensely. This may include heightened awareness of sights, sounds, textures, and subtle emotional or energetic signals. While such sensitivity can feel overwhelming in chaotic environments, it often enhances creativity, empathy, and intuition. Many neurodivergent individuals who experience sensory hypersensitivity may find that it significantly shapes how they interact with their surroundings, such as feeling distressed by noises, distractions, or visual stimuli that neurotypical individuals might not notice. Managing this sensitivity often requires conscious effort to regulate energy and sensory input, transforming it into a source of insight and authentic expression rather than a limitation.

The Toll of Masking

For many neurodivergent individuals, navigating a world shaped by neurotypical norms involves what's known as "masking", the effortful suppression of authentic behaviors to fit in. This performance, whether forcing eye contact or feigning attentiveness, demands significant mental energy. Juggling this effort alongside the social complexities of a traditional full-time job, managing personalities, office dynamics, and customer interactions, can lead to significant exhaustion. Rather than fostering connection, social engagement often becomes draining, leaving little energy for personal well-being. From my own experience, I've found that masking exacts a heavy physical and mental toll. Moving toward authentic expression has become a healing journey, supported by tools like the Energetic Resonance Effect and internal regulation practices, which help me reclaim my energy and connect more genuinely with others.

This systemic friction, the unrelenting pressure to conform, is the direct result of a prevailing corporate culture that actively punishes any type of divergence from the expected norm.

Corporate America and Neurodivergence: A Fundamental Mismatch

The structure of corporate America creates a systemic mismatch for neurodivergent individuals. Their essential needs for autonomy, flexibility, and genuine self-expression clash with the dominant corporate culture characterized by rigid hierarchies, uniform procedures, constant surveillance, and strict control. In this oppressive environment, compliance is enforced through fear and the looming threat of retaliation, with even routine personal decisions requiring formal approval. This intense regulation forces neurodivergent employees into chronic masking, the exhaustive suppression of their authentic selves, which rapidly increases stress, erodes trust, and stifles innovation.

For many neurodivergent individuals, this experience is not just difficult but unbearable, fundamentally undermining their ability to thrive. The relentless pressure to conform and the pervasive atmosphere of control strip away psychological safety and individuality.

Consequently, such environments do more than hinder everyday functioning, they extinguish their transformative potentials unique to neurodivergent minds, such as the capacity for resilience, insight, and creative growth through processes like E.R.E. Instead of nurturing these strengths, corporate culture's relentless control traps neurodivergent talent in a damaging cycle of chronic stress and burnout. The result is a loss for both the individual autonomy, left debilitated, and the organization, deprived of groundbreaking innovation and meaningful contributions, all sacrificed to a culture that prioritizes conformity over authentic diversity.

Recovery Time After Socializing for Neurodivergent Individuals

After social interactions, neurodivergent individuals often require a period of recovery to regulate their nervous system. This is not a matter of choice but a necessary process, especially following conversations or activities that demand significant social masking, consciously or unconsciously mimicking neurotypical behaviors, which can be mentally intense. Recovery typically involves solitude or spending time in a quiet, low-stimulus environment, allowing them to recharge their mental energy and detach from the experience.

Understanding Neurodivergence Hyper-focus Fatigue

Neurodivergent individuals often become absorbed in projects, sometimes working for long stretches without taking breaks. For example, a neurodivergent writer might spend 12 hours straight finishing a manuscript, or a hobbyist might devote an entire weekend to assembling a complex model, neglecting meals, rest, and sleep. This intense concentration can be mentally exhausting and often leads to feelings of fatigue and overwhelm. While this experience is commonly described as "neurodivergent burnout," that term does not fully capture the phenomenon. Traditional burnout usually refers to a gradual loss of motivation and interest due to chronic stress. In contrast, I prefer to call it **Neurodivergent Hyper-focus Fatigue**, which I feel better describes the sudden and complete depletion of energy that follows a period of sustained, intense focus. This term highlights the unique drain caused by hyper-focus, a specific exhaustion that comes not from disengagement but from concentrated effort.

70

The Struggle with Self-Limiting Beliefs

As a result of these constant struggles, some neurodivergent individuals develop intensely strong self-limiting beliefs, feeling a disconnect between their desires and their perceived abilities. This can manifest as an unwavering sense of imposter syndrome, where past challenges or negative experiences are internalized as definitive proof of their limitations. This unfortunate mindset can prevent many neurodivergent from taking risks, pursuing their passions, or even recognizing their own strengths, ultimately blocking them from realizing their full potential and the dreams they hold for themselves.

Non-Conformity: Distinguishing Trait from Behavior

Neurodivergent non-conformity arises organically from a neurological mismatch between the individual and a predominantly neurotypical environment. It is not a conscious act of rebellion or defiance, but rather a vital adaptation, a form of self-preservation. Because of this, the focus should move away from judging or controlling the behaviors it produces and instead toward recognizing and accommodating the underlying trait and its needs.

Unique Strengths: Pattern Recognition and Details

Despite the internal and external challenges, many neurodivergent people possess unique strengths. For instance, they excel at pattern recognition and attention to detail, giving them a unique advantage in problem-solving. This isn't just about spotting a repeating sequence; it's a form of hyper-observational awareness that goes beyond the surface. Their brains may be wired to process information in a more granular way, allowing them to spot subtle inconsistencies, minute discrepancies, or hidden relationships between data points. This ability isn't limited to data, it can manifest as an uncanny ability to read a room or spot social incongruities that others often miss. This focus on intricate details and the ability to find patterns where none are obvious can lead to highly creative and unconventional solutions that a more "big picture" thinker might never consider. Ultimately, this skill set is often not a conscious effort but a inherent byproduct of how many neurodivergent brains are wired to process the world.

This heightened perception doesn't end with the external world, it reaches into the intricate layers of emotion and energetics, where intuition forms in response to life's subtle signals. Many neurodivergent individuals experience the world in rich detail, a quality that often becomes a unique social strength: an ability to sense truth beneath the surface. While neurotypical people may rely on broader context or familiar social shortcuts, neurodivergent minds often process information from the ground up. This deep focus, shaped by heightened sensitivity or the need to make sense of a complex social world, helps them pick up on cues others might overlook. Shifts in tone, fleeting expressions, micro expression's, or tiny changes in body language can reveal volumes.

This finely tuned awareness often cultivates a strong sense of authenticity, enabling them to detect when words and energy are out of sync. What others call a "gut feeling" is, in fact, the neurodivergent mind sifting through countless subtle cues, forming remarkably accurate insights into someone's true state or intent.

How Neurodivergent Individuals Excel at Reading a Room
Many neurodivergent individuals possess an unusually sharp and often instinctive ability to "read a room," extending far beyond typical social awareness. Because they process social information differently, sometimes needing to consciously decode cues that others absorb effortlessly, they often develop a refined sensitivity to emotional and energetic authenticity. This depth of perception can translate into a strong attunement to others' energies, as they notice the subtle shifts in tone, posture, and micro-expressions that reveal underlying emotion. Their detailed, pattern-oriented observation can resemble a "sixth sense," allowing them to perceive with striking accuracy who feels and acts genuine and who does not.

This ability often emerges as a survival adaptation: having once missed or misread surface-level social interactions, they learn to trust, nonverbal signals and nuanced incongruities to gauge a person's true intent. Over time, this sustained focus cultivates an exceptional social finesse, a subtle, intuitive insight into human dynamics and the underlying character of those around them.

The Value of Expression for Neurodivergent Individuals
Another distinctive strength of neurodivergent individuals is the development of enhanced imaginative abilities, often serving as a powerful compensatory tool. Research increasingly shows that these creative strengths emerge from adapting to a world designed for a different neurology. This unique wiring allows individuals to perceive and experience their surroundings in ways that inherently lend themselves to artistic and creative pursuits (Miller, 2022). Rather than framing these differences as deficits, emphasizing strengths fosters resilience and the capacity to overcome challenges, highlighting that what makes a mind different often makes its imagination extraordinary.

Roots of Self: Neurodivergent Living Authentically
Neurodivergent authenticity means living in ways that match one's natural thinking, sensory needs, and social styles rather than bearing the comprehensive and unsustainable burden of constantly hiding or adapting to neurotypical expectations. Practically, this looks like choosing work, routines, and social settings that actively reduce the need for masking, using communication and accommodation strategies that fit individual needs, and prioritizing self-care that acknowledges sensory and executive differences. When daily life, relationships, employment, health, and leisure, reflects those needs, mental

health and a sense of belonging improve and energy that used to go toward masking can be redirected toward meaningful activity.

Transforming Masking with the Energetic Resonance Effect

Harnessing the Energetic Resonance Effect offers a transformative path beyond masking. This practice involves consciously shifting your internal energy by introducing a higher, more positive vibration that transforms and elevates lower, unsettled energies, a technique I previously introduced: the Superimposition Principle. By intentionally engaging in this energetic shift, individuals can express their authentic selves more freely and confidently, reducing the need to suppress natural behaviors to fit external expectations. This growth in authenticity creates a stronger connection between inner experience and outward expression, lessening the mental strain caused by masking. Using the B.E.T.E.R. framework, a simple, five-step process, you can cultivate your energetic state to make social interactions more genuine and less draining. This empowers you to conserve energy, encourage connections that honor your true identity, and build lasting emotional resilience and well-being.

Harnessing Superimposition for Authentic Connection

This shift toward self-preservation often leads to the development of distinctive coping mechanisms, such as adopting creative solutions to address these challenges. This is where the Authentic Magnetic Essence (AME) and the Energetic Resonance Effect (ERE) come into play, offering a unique avenue for wordless communication. The basis for this is the Superimposition Principle, which allows you to actively and consciously change your internal state. For example, when feeling anxious about a necessary but unwanted obligation, you can superimpose an optimistic viewpoint over the pessimistic feelings. Instead of focusing on discomfort or angst, you can divert your attention by engaging in something uplifting, like listening to music or taking a walk. This new energy then softens and dissolves the negative feelings connected to what was troubling you. Shifting focus from external interpretation to internal acceptance provides a more direct and authentic way to connect with others, reducing the pressure to navigate neurotypical communication styles.

The Upgraded Nervous System

Some modern metaphysical thinkers propose a radically different view of neurodivergence, moving away from the idea of a deficit. They suggest that the neurodivergent nervous system is not flawed, but rather hyper-capable and highly sensitive, likening it to an advanced system receiving excessive information without clear instructions for management. The result is often the well-known experience of overload, overwhelm, and burnout, even when physically resting. This perspective reframes the difficulty as an environmental mismatch, the system is processing a high volume of environmental stimuli and energy that standard societal environments are not designed to accommodate. From this viewpoint, the exhaustion felt in crowded public settings stems from the sheer volume of sensory data as well other people's energy being processed by the neurodivergent person. This highly intensive processing demands extra resources, possibly accounting for the frequent need for readily available energy sources, such as glucose. The path to ease, according to this theory, is not in trying to fix the system, but in learning to condition and support this powerful level of sensitivity.

The Upgrade

How might society shift its view of neurodivergence from a deficit to a complex, sophisticated adaptation? Imagine a mind tuned to a different, more powerful frequency, one capable of hyper-observation that reveals hidden patterns and connections. This brain processes information not in a linear fashion, but through a creative, multi-layered lens that generates innovative solutions a neurotypical mind might overlook. While living in a society designed for neurotypicality can be challenging and painful, consider that traits often seen as sources of friction, such as unfiltered honesty and heightened emotional sensitivity, may actually represent more direct and effective ways of engaging with the world. Seen through this lens, the distinctive ways in which some individuals interact with their environment might be exactly the adaptations society needs to inspire fresh ideas and creative problem solving. What is often mistaken for weakness could, in truth, be a hidden super power.

A Journey of Resilience for Neurodivergent Individuals

Ultimately, adapting to a world designed for neurotypical individuals cultivates resilience in neurodivergent people, transforming pain into a vital tool for navigating life's demands. This resilience often manifests as unique coping strategies that also serve as strengths, such as innovative thinking, intense focus, and exceptional attention to detail. By drawing on this inner strength to overcome challenges, neurodivergent individuals develop not only the ability to survive but also to thrive as innovators, leaders, and pioneers in their fields. Their journey is marked by continual growth, self-discovery, and empowering transformation, demonstrating that difference often fuels greatness.

Reflective Question

In what ways have you had to reclaim parts of your identity or personal perspective that might not fit societal expectations?

Chapter Summary: This chapter offers a rich exploration of neurodivergence as a fundamentally different way of processing the world, an alternative "operating system" for the brain. It highlights the unique challenges faced by neurodivergent individuals, including sensory sensitivities, the exhaustive toll of masking, and the frequent mismatch with rigid social expectations. A key focus is the social friction of first impressions, explaining why neurodivergent communication styles often lead to initial unease or resistance from neurotypical people. The chapter also addresses common struggles with social norms, communication styles, and self-limiting beliefs that arise from living in a world built primarily for neurotypical functioning. Despite these obstacles, the chapter celebrates distinctive neurodivergent strengths such as exceptional pattern recognition, intuitive perception, and creative imagination, revealing how these capacities foster authenticity, resilience, and innovation. Ultimately, it calls for a societal shift away from pathologizing difference toward embracing neurodiversity as a source of wisdom and transformative growth.

To conclude this chapter on the Oblique Angle, this poem frames neurodivergence not as a flaw, but as a heightened sensitivity and an upgraded system for receiving the world.

The Veiled Meridian

I hold a sensor, wired and bright,
A nervous system tuned to light.
Not flawed or broken but refined,
An upgrade in the human mind.

The world perceives a deficit,
Where in my core a flame is lit.
They misread the vast demand
Of every signal I command.

The street, the mall, the open din,
A thousand lives are pouring in.
I take the sound, the flicker, glow,
The pulsing stream of all I know.

The collective rhythm, fast and deep,
While others talk, I watch, I keep
The endless ledger of the air,
The silent hum of hidden care.

My brain consumes the boundless plain,
A burning engine needing drain
Of glucose, ATP, the fire
That feeds this live electric wire.

The overload, the burnout's sting,
Don't come from sloth or weakening,
But from the quiet truth I keep,
A mask upon a charge too deep.

So hold this vision, clear and keen:
The power of what has been seen.
This depth, this heightened inner sight,
Not a flaw, but future light.

Chapter VII: The Charged Loom: Self-Honor and Energetic Boundaries

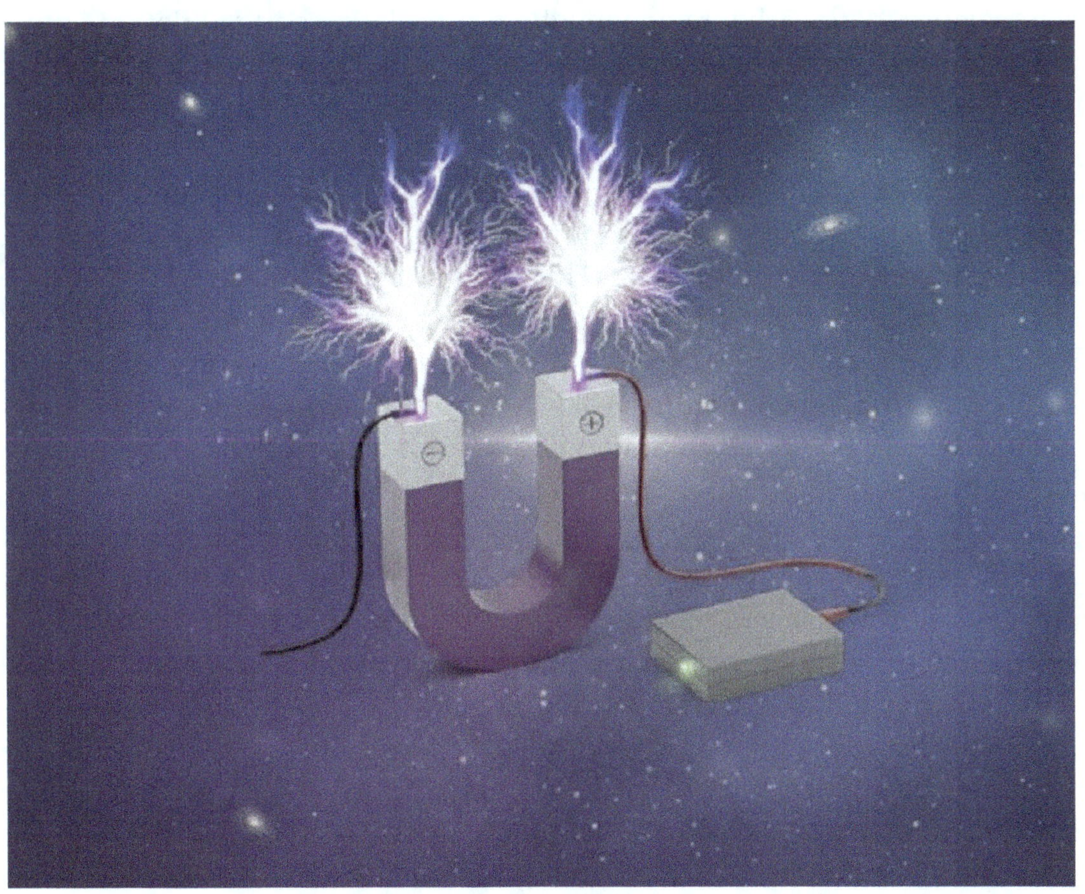

Figure 7.1: An electro-magnet recharges when connected to power, symbolizing the process of **ENERGETIC MAGNETIZATION** and the deliberate renewal of your internal magnetism.

When I embody the Energetic Resonance Effect, I become a living beacon, a subtle yet powerful force that reshapes the space around me through magnetic presence. This energy is not accidental; it is born of intention: a vivid testament that we need not settle for lives marked by disconnection, depletion, or numbing routine. My purpose is to embody enduring vitality, inviting others to witness the possibilities that arise when we stay grounded in our inner radiance.

However, this radiance inevitably draws others in, revealing what I call The **Reciprocity Deficit**. People are quick to seek out and bask in your elevated frequency, drawing inspiration, excitement, and renewal from what I freely radiate. Too often, however, they leave behind a void where reciprocity could be. The exchange falters; my energy becomes a resource consumed rather than honored and reciprocated, a one-way current that creates imbalance. With each interaction where stimulation and validation flow only outward, resentment can be to creep in , dimming the brightness with fatigue and disillusionment.

I cannot be a constant wellspring for others' fleeting elevation, nor should my presence be treated as a spectacle to dispel their emptiness. Sustaining this lopsided exchange erodes ones vitality, creating an energetic cost. This calls for compassionate boundaries and conscious mutuality that honor both giving and receiving of energy. Recognizing this pattern means I am required to actively protect my energetic resource. My vitality is not a public utility; true alignment requires prioritizing self-preservation over perpetual availability. The goal is to keep shining without allowing that light to become an open invitation for unchecked consumption by others.

Setting compassionate boundaries to shield my energetic source becomes essential. Prioritizing vitality as a sacred resource ensures continued radiance without becoming a "loophole for consumption," paving the way for relationships grounded in conscious mutuality rather than habitual extraction.

In this journey, monitoring internal patterns, such as excessive worry, fear, self-criticism, gossip, or reactive conflict, is essential. Reducing these energetic drains is crucial for preserving your reserves and sustaining your radiant presence.

Practices for Energetic Upliftment: Cultivating Magnetized Authenticity.
This chapter shares suggestions and practices that have helped me strengthen my transmutational skills, the ability to intentionally shift energy, and enhance the Energetic Resonance Effect, a method for uplifting and energizing oneself. Central to this process is something I call **Energetic Magnetization**: the deliberate practice of recharging your

internal magnetism to draw in aligned experiences. Incorporating these techniques has significantly improved my capacity to engage with and embody higher energetic states.

Authenticity acts as a clear channel for your life force, amplifying your natural magnetism. By embracing what makes you unique, light and shadow alike, you reinforce the core of your Energetic Magnetization. The more genuine and honest you become, the more balanced and powerful your energy field grows. This self-alignment is essential not only for sustaining the Energetic Resonance Effect but also for maintaining the magnetic charge that draws your desired experiences toward you.

Nurturing Your Energetic State

To sustain a vibrant energetic presence, you should tend faithfully to your inner landscape. Release stagnant emotions such as grief, anger, fear, and sadness, as they will disrupt your flow and keep you tethered to your past. Practice self-forgiveness for what has been, recognizing that you acted with the awareness you had at the time. Remain hopeful, even amid difficulty; the future holds infinite potential. And finally, use humor to stay light and present, it keeps your energy playful, radiant, and free.

Building Sustainable Practices

Change requires consistency and repetition. Establish a routine and consistently practice these techniques to improve your ability to access the Energetic Resonance Effect. Avoid pushing yourself to exhaustion through over-work; take breaks and rest when necessary to allow your body and energy to recharge. When negative emotions arise, bounce back quickly by shifting your attention before they gain momentum. To become more effective at energetic transmutation, focus your energy on the feelings you want to cultivate and release the ones you don't. For example, if you feel anxious, consciously focus on feeling calm.

Intentional Connection with the World

Your energetic presence is influenced by how you engage with others and your environment. Do what you enjoy, as this effortlessly helps you tap into your transmutational abilities. When you're having fun, things fall into place much more easily, helping you enter a state of flow. Cultivate a thankful mindset for the good things in your life to attract even more of what you desire. Spend time alone to reconnect with yourself and ensure your path remains in line with your intentions. Finally, learn from others by observing how they trigger you, as this can reveal your own internal blind spots and offer valuable insights for self improvement and growth.

Potential Obstacles

Becoming a more effective energetic practitioner requires you to navigate the common obstacles that can block your energetic flow. The following are internal and external barriers to be aware of and overcome.

Internal Obstacles

These are the mental and emotional barriers that originate from within and can stifle your energetic abilities.

- **The Cynicism Barrier**: Cynicism creates a mental filter that dismisses or diminishes the very language you're trying to transmute, short-circuiting the process before it can begin. The cynical mind questions any change, which makes it nearly impossible to transform concepts from thoughts into felt experiences. To overcome this, temporarily suspend your cynical tendencies and engage with new ideas from a place of curiosity, openness and curiosity rather than with doubt and cynicism.

- **Self-Doubt**: Self-doubt is a dream killer that can instill feelings of hopelessness. This type of negative self-talk will block your transformational abilities and interfere with your energetic practice. To counteract this, stay aware of your internal dialogue and actively replace any self-doubts with self encouragement.

- **The Need for External Validation**: Seeking acceptance and validation from others is an exercise in futility. Genuine acceptance must come from within. Only by embracing and accepting who you truly are can you diminish any feelings of unworthiness.

The Downward Spiral

The Downward Spiral is what I call a progression fueled by a negative mindset. The loss of hope can quickly lead to feelings of despair and discouragement. Once these emotions take root and set in, they pull us deeper into a cycle of powerlessness, having us believe there is no solution possible for our problems. This in turn leads us to give up on ourselves, which only reinforces a pattern of self defeat. Left unchecked, despair becomes a destructive force that continually increases our sense of hopelessness and low self worth.

The Negativity Loop

This powerful, negative mindset of shame and self-rejection sets off a dangerous cycle. It's like falling into quicksand; the more we reason with it, fight it, or even give it attention, the stronger its pull becomes. I call this a **Negativity Loop**, and digging ourselves out takes a lot of energy. We can better help ourselves by stopping this process before it becomes a powerfully self-perpetuating pattern. The universal law of "like attracts like" kicks in, drawing more negativity into our lives until we find ourselves trapped in a downward spiral of incredibly painful experiences and extremely difficult to escape.

~ If you believe your life doesn't matter, that you are not needed, you become your own worst enemy.

When this negativity loop takes hold, it transforms emotion into a fragile prison, each thought a pane in a glass cage, reflecting missed moments and unspoken wounds.

Grief Lodged in Glass

Glass cage, you haunt me.
Each pane, a ghost of missed moments.
My heart gasps,
life's touch slips past.

Fear binds me
within the frame I built,
pane by pane,
trembling hands, so carefully.

I ache for the world beyond,
lost lessons,
unclaimed laughter,
love untouched.

Through this clear barrier,
life flows past.
Close enough to feel,
too far to reach.

Is freedom mine?
Where does strength arise
to shatter this flawless cage?

How does one unmake
what was built so carefully,
grief lodged in glass?

Breaking the Cycle

Have you ever noticed that when we constantly think about, talk about, or worry about a problem, it never seems to get resolved? In fact, the issue just festers and lingers. This happens because our energy, fueled by worry, fear, or rumination, sustains the problem, allowing it to persist. To break this cycle, we must stop feeding our problems this attention. We can counter feelings of despair by intentionally shifting our mindset. Since the future is unknown, why not choose optimism over pessimism? When we expect good outcomes, we tend to focus less on negativity, which actually improves our chances of success. By pulling our energy away from destructive mindsets, we open space for constructive solutions to appear. We can start reframing the situation right now to help break this cycle.

Practicing the Energetic Resonance Effect

We can use the Energetic Resonance Effect to override these negative thought patterns. While it may seem counterintuitive, by deliberately adopting an optimistic perspective, we can begin to shift our focus to a bigger, less bleak picture that is more open to improved changes. The key is to start before we reach a point of "no return" and get trapped in a **Negativity Loop**. It's important to revisit and challenge the negative beliefs that may be contributing to our despair. Identifying and confronting these limiting beliefs can help us break free from cycles of negativity, enabling us to shift our mindset and embrace more self empowering beliefs.

The Self-Honor Principle

One truth I eventually came to understand is that self-compassion is the most crucial act for my well-being: mentally, physically, socially, and energetically. As a child, and even into adulthood, I believed that if only I felt more loved my pain would vanish. The reality I came to understand is that the only person who can truly care for me is myself. I call this the **Self-Honor Principle**. It is the transformative realization that self-compassion is the most crucial act for our well-being. This clear understanding that only we can genuinely care for ourselves becomes the greatest gift we can give ourselves, as it allows us to build a foundation of self-respect and stop the cycle of self-rejection.

To embody the Self-Honor Principle and actively foster self-compassion, we can engage in focused emotional work. The following practice uses the power of intentional breathing and verbal transmutation to transform heavy emotion into self healing energy.

Transforming Heavy Emotion into Self Healing Energy

Take a moment to center yourself and be aware of how you feel in this moment. Allow yourself to identify three or four words that capture any emotions weighing on you, such as worry, fear, sadness, or anger.

With these feelings named, breathe in and speak a mantra that transforms these negative energies into something nurturing. Speak aloud with intention and presence:

"I transmute all worry, fear, negativity, and self-criticism into self-compassion and self healing."

Repeat this mantra, allowing each word to resonate. See if you will start to notice the burden of these emotions begins to shift, and if your energy begins to start moving toward relief.

Energetic Contractions

These are energies that actively work against the flow you are trying to cultivate, causing you to contract rather than expand.

- **Brooding**: Unlike constructive energy that expands and radiates, brooding is a quiet, contracting force that carries resentment and suppressed anger. This dense emotional field creates negative tension in the space, acting in opposition to the Energetic Resonance Effect and subtly blocking positive movement and change.

- **Complaining**: Complaining takes you out of your confidence and puts you in a state of helplessness. It blocks your ability to transmute the Energetic Resonance Effect and burdens those around you. Instead of complaining, focus on things you prefer to reclaim your power and elevate your energy.

- **Stress**: Stress is an inevitable part of life, but unmanaged stress will take you out of your ability to be an effective practitioner of the E.R.E. Finding ways to reduce and manage stress is essential for maintaining life balance and keeping your energetic abilities strong.

Societal and Lifestyle Barriers:

These external pressures and habits can hinder your progress and affect your energetic flow:

- **Conformity**: The pressure to conform damages your individuality, creativity and authenticity. When you squash your unique qualities to fit in, you lose access to the very qualities that make you an interesting individual. Conformity discourages and inhibits original thinking.

- **Overextending**: You cannot be in a perpetual state of rushing around and expect to become a more effective transmuter. This constant overexertion stifles your abilities. It's in slowing down and refraining from pushing yourself too hard that you accelerate your ability to become a better practitioner of E.R.E.

Navigating Unintended Reflections

As you cultivate your internal power, your energetic field will strengthen, and others may begin to notice. This can lead to a couple of unintended social side effects that are important to be aware of. The first is when your personal energy is misread, a phenomenon I call **Energetic Misinterpretation**. As you practice the Energetic Resonance Effect, you are channeling energy back into yourself. What others are sensing is the radiant, self-directed charge you are cultivating. They may mistake this internal focus for a directed attraction toward them, which can sometimes lead to awkward or uncomfortable situations, especially if the attention is unwanted.

The second is a phenomenon I call **Reflective Confidence**. Have you ever noticed how someone's genuine self-assurance can make others uneasy or defensive? This isn't born from arrogance or a desire to show off, but rather from an unconscious mirroring effect. The confident person's secure presence reflects back the observer's own perceived insecurities, serving as a mirror for their self-doubt. This can often result in others feeling bothered, defensive, or irritated by your confident state, even when your intentions are benign. The overall effect of this practice is always elevating for the confident person. For the observer, this reflection can be a complicated experience; the trigger of seeing someone content in their own skin may feel annoying to some. However, for a person who is ready to grow, witnessing another's authentic self-assurance can be a helpful and inspiring example of what's possible for them.

Conclusion

By embracing these positive practices and consciously navigating potential obstacles, you can cultivate a stronger connection to your own power and enhance your ability to communicate energetically.

Reflective Questions:

Of the practices outlined, which one do you feel you are already using effectively, and what does that tell you about your current energetic state?

What is one specific problem or negative thought pattern you've been "feeding" with your energy, and what is one small step you can take today to stop giving it that attention?

Chapter Summary: This chapter explores Energetic Magnetization, the intentional recharging of inner energy to attract aligned people, circumstances, and opportunities, offering uplifting practices to cultivate an authentic core, overcome blocks like doubt and conformity, and recognize the destructive pull of the Downward Spiral and Negativity Loop. The poem Grief Lodged in Glass illustrates the paralysis of fear and the longing for release. Through the Self-Honor Principle, readers learn that self-compassion dissolves cycles of shame and restores energetic flow, strengthening personal power and communication.

Chapter VIII: The Silent Ebb: Clearing Energetic Slop

Figure 8.1: **Energetic Slop**: The Habitual Mismanagement of One's Energy

Figure 8.1: Energetic Slop: A surreal, central figure composed of organic matter and mechanical gears, featuring a hollow chest and serving as a hub for numerous floating digital devices connected by glowing lines. Root-like tendrils extend from this being toward tablets displaying data, set against a backdrop of a blurred crowd and two foreground men absorbed in their smartphones. Standing upon cracked, desolate earth, the scene visualizes the complex relationship between humanity and the digital world, highlighting themes of connectivity and data consumption.

The Silent Ebb: Clearing Energetic Slop

When we think of someone who constantly wastes energy through excessive worry, nonstop talking, chronic fear, negativity, or unnecessary drama, the draining impact becomes clear. These behaviors chip away at our inner vitality, leaving us scattered, depleted, and disconnected from ourselves. I call this **Energetic Slop**: a metaphorical junk drawer where habitual energy mismanagement accumulates as unaddressed frustrations, worries, fears, stress, overthinking and over talking. As this clutter builds, it spills into every corner of daily life, conversations, inner dialogue, and environmental distractions, making balance elusive. This depletion scatters focus and fosters persistent unrest within.

The intentional reduction of Energetic Slop is vital for restoring focus and vitality. These seemingly minor poor habits, when repeated, weave patterns that gradually drain our energy. Whether caught in interpersonal drama, distracted by constant noise, or locked in unhelpful routines, the outcome is the same: an accumulation of Energetic Slop. It leaves us ungrounded, unfocused, and increasingly susceptible to stress and dissatisfaction.

Unfortunately, this condition is widespread today. Walk through any public space, and you'll see people stuck in the cycle, lost in digital devices, trapped in endless internal chatter, or overwhelmed by surrounding noise and distractions.

The Tyranny of Distraction

Our culture has become obsessed with distraction. Quiet moments now feel uncomfortable, often needing to fill them with idle chatter, scrolling, streaming, or swiping. It's as if we've forgotten how to feel at ease without constant noise and stimulation. This continuous stream of input often masks bigger issues: restlessness, a fear of stillness, or a craving for validation. Many seek approval through social media likes, comments, and endless conversation, trying to fill a void that can only be addressed from within.

Distractions like smartphones and social media are ever-present. But it wasn't long ago that we lived without this constant influx of idle chatter. Once, we were less distracted and more in tune with ourselves. Now, these distractions have dulled our senses, lulled our awareness, and thinned our connection to what truly matters: our inner peace, sense of well-being and internal energetic signature. This pervasive influence ultimately saps our energy.

Reflective Question
Where might you be unconsciously "sloppy" with your energy?

Chapter Summary: This chapter introduces Energetic Slop, the habitual mismanagement of personal energy, reflected in patterns such as chronic worry, negativity, overthinking, fear and unnecessary drama. Beyond digital devices and social media, distraction seeps into mental chatter, relationship conflicts, and environmental noise.

This state, the loss of presence amidst the noise, is the essence of the walking trance. The poem that follows attempts to capture this hypnotic condition and the faint, enduring call to awaken and truly perceive.

A Walking Trance

They drift beneath the veil of sleep,

Along the paths the silent keep.

Their eyes are closed against the light,

As false beliefs obscure their sight.

Their vital strength begins to fade;

Through shadowed depths their footsteps wade.

Through hollow halls where echoes call,

They trace each cold, unfeeling wall.

They breathe the air of endless gloom,

Within the sleeper's shadowed tomb.

The grinding system starts to hum,

Relentless, calling them to come,

To merge, dissolve into the stream,

As wanes the soul's once-guiding gleam.

Yet past the pounding, vacant sound,

A single, steady breath is found.

So soft it splits the trance in two,

Revealing all that's bright and new,

A molten hope begins to rise,

To clear the blindfold from their eyes,

To wake the soul to clarity,

To sudden, vast lucidity.

Chapter IX: Echoes of Future: Reclaiming Imagination with Theta Wave

Figure 9.1: The journey from routine to reverie begins with a single shift.

Figure 9.1: Shows a split image on the left, a grayscale adult surrounded by dark industrial gears represents a tired, monotonous routine. On the right, a vibrant child gazes through a telescope at a colorful, whimsical city under a sky with clouds and floating books, symbolizing creative wonder. Connecting them in the center, an open book emits a glowing blue stream with rocket ships and light elements, blending steampunk and fantasy to contrast dull routine with vibrant imagination.

Gone in a flash

And in a flash, it was gone,

that childhood gleam in your eyes

now just a flicker.

Dreams worn thin

on the gears of routine.

Weeks bleed into one another,

a carousel of work,

each day a drip of time

that drains you.

A cog made to produce,

one gear in an endless machine.

"What's the point?" you ask

in quiet desperation,

as your heart cries out

to ears that will not listen,

not even your own.

So worn, so run down,

that when the torch is passed,

the life you were promised,

you're too spent to hold it.

You whisper to the past,

"Was it all worth it?"

Echoes in Future

Somewhere between childhood wonder and adult routine, a part of you got lost. You once built castles in the air, sailed imaginary seas, and believed in the impossible. Now, that magic feels buried beneath the relentless rhythm of deadlines and to-do lists. But what if the magic was never lost? What if you forgot how to access the playful awe and open-hearted curiosity that once fueled your imagination and transformation?

The key lies in rediscovering your brain's remarkable ability to shape and transmute, transmuting, your preferred future through a state called theta. That childlike wonder you cherish isn't just innocent play, it reflects your brain entering the theta state, where imagination, intuition, and inner shifts converge. As children, we slip effortlessly into this space, but as adults, we often lose touch with it. Without practice, this potent power fades.

I call this **Theta Wave Transmutational Imagination**. Neuroscience reveals that theta waves, oscillating between 3.5 and 7.5 Hz, bridge conscious thought and the subconscious mind. In this state, your mind opens to intuitive insights, vivid daydreams, and energetic transformation of limiting beliefs into fresh possibilities. Boosting theta activity enhances creativity, reduces stress, and unlocks a gateway where old patterns dissolve, making way for new mental blueprints infused with childlike wonder and transformative potential.

Reclaiming Your Imaginative Power

Your imagination shapes your life, offering a vision of what could be and letting you mentally live what doesn't yet exist. The theta state is the fertile soil where these visions take root, grow stronger, and manifest. To harness this power, combine the vivid imagery of childlike awe with the transformative capacity of theta-enhanced states. For example, before a big presentation, instead of just rehearsing, enter a theta-enhanced imaginative space, see yourself walking in confidently, feel the excitement of your colleagues, and absorb their praise. This felt experience plants a transformational seed, increasing the likelihood your vision will become reality.

This intimate dance between imagination and theta waves, theta enhanced imagination, is a personal, transmutational practice. With intention and practice, it becomes a powerful tool to rediscover creativity, transform limiting patterns, and manifest a future filled with wonder and possibility.

Reflective Question: What childhood dream or passion have you set aside, and how might reclaiming your imaginative thinking in a theta state help you rediscover and pursue it today?

Chapter Summary: This chapter explores the transformative power of Theta Wave Transmutational Imagination, a unique state where the brain's theta waves merge with vibrant imaginative focus to unlock deep inner change. It reveals how this natural brain rhythm acts as a bridge between conscious awareness and the subconscious, creating fertile ground for creative visualization, intuitive insights, and the energetic transmutation of limiting beliefs. Readers will learn how to access and cultivate this state to reshape mental patterns, ignite personal growth, and manifest a future rich with possibility and wonder. Through practical examples and reflective prompts, the chapter invites a rediscovery of the imaginative power that fuels transformation and renewal.

~ The genie was never in the bottle. It was always in you.

The Sovereign's Price

I did not come to stand here, still and cold,
A hollow casing for a tale untold.
No circuit board or metal frame is mine,
To serve their bottom line, a grim design.
I am not here to be utilized and spent,
A mere automaton for their intent;
A single cog for their machines to seize,
And drain the last reserves of what is me.
The meager wages, a calculated slight,
Enough to keep the flickering wick alight.
To stave off hunger, pay the monthly due,
To barely grasp the thread of living through.
But in return, a steep and cruel exchange,
I lose my sovereign, wild and vital range,
My peace is fractured, and my health grows weary,
Consumed before the workday's light turns dreary.
That vital freedom, always out of sight,
A shifting mirage in fluorescent light.
I did not come to trade away my soul,
To fuel the profits and surrender control.
While stock traders cheer and fortunes grow,
And those at the peak ascend their towers of glass,
I am the fuel that burns itself, alas,
Depleted, directionless, at close of day.
The threat hangs heavy, waiting to descend,
The wrong word spoken, and the contract ends.
A silent censure, walls that close me in,
Confining spirit where true life begins.
And when my purpose is considered done,
I'm cast aside, their victory won,

A piece of wreckage left upon the shore.
I am disposable, and nothing more.

Chapter X: Pulse of the Unseen: Meditation for Energetic Stability

Figure 10.1: Stillness and motion lead to clarity.

Figure 10:1 A silhouetted figure meditating, from whom blue and gold energy flows out, connecting to several dualistic symbols. These symbols include interlocked spirals, figures running toward creative tools versus nature scenes, and a path featuring a lightbulb (ideas) and gears (logic). This composition conveys a theme of harmony and the balance between inner peace, different thought processes, and outward aspects of life.

Pulse of the Unseen: Meditation for Energetic Stability
Traditional Meditation and Alternative Practices
Meditation can take many forms, depending on how we connect to silence and awareness. One method is traditional meditation: sitting in stillness with eyes closed, observing thoughts without judgment. This helps to slow down a restless mind.

For those who prefer movement or creativity over stillness, alternative practices can be just as effective. Activities like creating art, playing sports, walking, or engaging in hobbies can also bring us into a meditative state. These practices focus the mind, quiet mental noise, and give the brain an opportunity to recalibrate and reset. They provide many of the same benefits as seated meditation without requiring complete stillness.

Taming an Overactive Ego
Quieting the mind through meditation also helps tame the overactive ego. At times, our ego can get the best of us. We may blame our problems on another person or an external situation. When this happens, our ego grows stronger as we justify our stance and repeatedly remind ourselves that someone or something else is completely responsible for our unhappiness. This cycle keeps us stuck, reinforcing a rigid perspective and preventing growth.

There is another way. We can choose to take ownership by acknowledging the role we may have played in creating a difficult situation while still meeting ourselves with compassion.

When you notice your ego starting to take over, repeat this mantra.
• I acknowledge I may have played a part in creating this situation.
• And I choose to respond with self-compassion and love towards myself.

By practicing ownership with self-compassion, we break harmful cycles of blame, calming the ego, and face challenges with greater kindness and constructive understanding toward both ourselves and others.

When You Feel Attacked

When someone attacks, criticizes, or belittles your character, your stance, your beliefs, or your values, repeat this short mantra to yourself until your emotions settle:

"I radiate and reflect back the energy of love."

In doing this you are transmuting their negativity in to something more beneficial for all involved.

This poem invites you to enter the quiet silence, celebrating the intuition and self-knowledge that emerge from stillness.

Pulse of the Unseen

In stillness, what's forgotten breathes,
A pulse from stars' intuited seas.

Silence unveils the ancient chord,
Where thought dissolves, where light is poured.

A golden lattice hums unseen,
It threads through souls that drift between.

Even shadow holds its grace,
A dance within the boundless space.

Along the unseen current, deep,
I wake, not searching, but to keep

The memory of that primal gleam
That dreamed my being into form.

Chapter XI: The Fear-Forged Flow: Transforming Resistance into Purpose

Figure 11.1: The energy of fear and resistance is not to be avoided, but transmuted! Its depth and darkness feed the brilliant, upward flow of growth and purpose.

Transforming Fear and Resistance into Purpose:
The Fear-Forged Flow
Fear often gets a bad reputation, but it is best viewed as a cloaked companion and messenger providing us with valuable insights we might otherwise overlook.

One of its benefits is that fear signals when something needs our attention. Fear manifests physically as discomfort, and this energy can become trapped in our physical body. This is our body's signal to gain our attention.

Rather than confront these fears, our first instinct is often to run from them, choosing a safer, more familiar path. This inaction is a form of self-betrayal. By suppressing or avoiding our fears, we allow them to grow more overwhelming, negatively affecting us physically, mentally, emotionally, and spiritually.

The River of Resistance
This instinct to avoid confrontation and choose inaction is precisely what creates unnecessary obstacles in our lives. When something obstructs a river's path, a fallen log, a dam, the water swells with frustrated force, bursting its banks and unleashing chaos. This overflowing mirrors the resistance we create in our own lives by building an inner dam against the reality of fear. When we introduce blockages through fear or the need to control each outcome, we add unnecessary suffering for ourselves. A rigid stance is like a dam we build within ourselves. The answers we seek are often revealed subtly, through ideas, thoughts, events and nudges. When we ignore these signs and dig into an inflexible position, and we only increase our problems.

Flowing Around the Companion
What if we chose allowance and intentional transmutation instead of resistance? We could stop struggling against the stream and grant ourselves permission to be guided by its course. We can transform this resistance using a mindful approach that shifts fear into purpose. This is where the practice of what I call **Energetic Fear Regulation** becomes essential. Energetic Fear Regulation is a practice of consciously transmuting fear's energy into a catalyst for positive action.

For example, when you feel the energy of fear rising in your body, instead of fleeing from it, pause and breathe into it, acknowledge it and any sensations it brings. Then, focus on the act of transmuting your fear in order to shift your internal state. This process does not dismiss fear but transforms it can weaken the energy behind it. Taking this alternate path may feel overwhelming initially when you are caught up in the moment, thus requiring greater initial effort. Yet, by choosing this approach, you may be able to cultivate a reduction in your fear response.

Chapter summary: The strength of a river is not found in its ability to be dammed, but in its persistent, flexible flow, the flow that, over time, can carve a canyon from solid rock. The principle is clear: what seems difficult today, the choice to move past the cloaked companion or the proverbial river of resistance, often becomes our greatest source of strength. In the end, what feels easy now may become harder later, while what seems difficult today often becomes our greatest source of strength and most significant source of growth.

The Fear-Forged Flow

From swirling depths of shadowed night,

Where black and purple clouds ignite,

A vibrant tree begins to rise,

Rooted deep, it claims the skies.

Fear, a cloaked companion near,

Whispers truths we strain to hear.

Not to flee, but face and feel,

Its fierce fire, the force to heal.

Resistance builds the river's dam,

Blocking strength we once could command.

Yet waters bend, persist, and climb,

Carving canyons through all time.

Breathe the dark, embrace the flame,

Transmute the fear, reclaim your name.

From chaos born, a steady light,

Fuel for growth, radiant and bright.

What once was wall becomes the flow,

Through hardest paths, let courage grow.

In every pulse, a lesson told,

From fearful ash, new life unfolds.

Chapter XII: The Abyss Compass: Breaking Limiting Beliefs

Figure 12.1 A visual representation of the **prison of our beliefs**

Figure 12.1: The conceptual image displays a translucent, silhouetted human figure standing on cracked earth, tightly constrained across the chest and waist by thick, dark, twisted ropes or wires. Flanking the figure are abstract elements of distress: a large, shattered piece of glass on the left with smoky tendrils, and dark, swirling vortexes on the right. An ominous dark cloud dominates the top of the scene, broken only by a glowing, fiery sun, creating a high-contrast visualization of struggle, constraint, and internal conflict.

The Prison of Beliefs

Our beliefs have immense influence over our outcomes. If we want something but believe we can't have it, it will always remain just out of reach. Our past experiences often shape these beliefs, often times leading us to unknowingly sabotage our own success.

These beliefs often go unnoticed because they operate below the surface. To break free, we need to understand their origins. When they become this instilled, I call them **Entrenched Beliefs**. They are psychological barriers that form when outdated self-perceptions become so fixed that they limit our efforts, constrain achievement, and prevent us from recognizing our current potential.

~ Discounting ourselves and our abilities is a missed opportunity to achieve something great.

To better capture the feeling of this unseen barrier, consider this poetic reflection on the constraint and willful blindness it imposes:

Veil of Compliance

A masquerade, a velvet hand,
a blindfold drawn across the land.
We gaze but never truly see,
unaware of all we'd be.
We dread the weight of asking why,
as shadows veil the narrowing sky.
Unseen, the binding chains remain,
the pattern whispers once again.
Unmoved, unquestioned, still we comply,
and tread the path they deify.
We never part the silken veil,
to sense the vastness dim and pale.
Obedient to ghostly might,
we barter voice to hold the night.
Bound by laws we did not writ,
our vision forged by borrowed light.
Do not question. Don't resist.
Do not wander past the mist.
The price of truth, a siren's charm,
is pain, stay warm within the calm.

This poem reflects the invisible yet powerful chains of our beliefs, how they limit our vision and trap us in cycles of obedience and compliance. Understanding this is the first step to breaking free and exploring the origins of our Entrenched Beliefs.

Transmuting Self-Rejection and Viral Limitations

I intimately know the cycle of self-rejection and self-imposed limitations. Early childhood experiences etched lasting impressions on my psyche, planting limiting beliefs that many of my deepest desires were out of reach. Success in certain areas felt like an impenetrable barrier, though I longed for something with all my heart, a part of me remained convinced it was unattainable and forever beyond my grasp.

In response, I discovered a transformative coping strategy: transmuting this self-rejection. Rather than letting failures drag me down, I learned to convert that pain into self-acceptance. This process involves embracing who you are right now, acknowledging past wounds, and using that awareness to forge a stronger future self.

The Allure of Giving Up

The temptation to give up often feels like a relief, freeing us from the pressure we once imposed on ourselves to keep pushing forward. Yet beneath this calm lies a deep fear. The real danger is adopting a defeated mindset, which traps us in a cycle of failure and disappointment driven by those hidden fears. This mindset resists stepping beyond the familiar safety of our comfort zones.

Our limiting beliefs harm not only ourselves but also others. When we express these constrained views aloud, we risk spreading a restrictive worldview. If others internalize this mindset, they too become trapped in the same limiting patterns. I call this **Viral Limitation**. Each time we voice these beliefs, they grow stronger within us and exert power over us and those who hear them spoken. However, with mindful awareness and self-restraint before speaking, we can interrupt this destructive cycle.

Beliefs shape how we perceive the world. Examining these often distorted beliefs reveals how we unknowingly block our own path to success. There are always reasons we cling to unwanted limitations, and uncovering them requires dedicated self-exploration.

Reflective question:

What belief have I accepted as a permanent truth, and what new possibilities would emerge if I allowed myself to outgrow it?

Forward Velocity and The Miscalculation

Forward velocity is in reference to our momentum, the driving force that propels us toward what we desire. The key to harnessing this force lies in taking action, no matter how small, toward our goals. Momentum serves as a catalyst, transforming intentions into reality. Without it, progress often remains stalled.

The very first step in the direction we want to go sets everything into motion. When we hesitate or fail to take inspired action, we send a clear signal to our psyche that the desire is unattainable.

This hesitation to move forward, even when we desire change, reveals an underlying force that can silently stall our progress. I call this force **Dormant Power,** a latent energy rooted in fear, complacency, and or self doubt that keeps us from taking inspired action. It is this Dormant Power that often masks itself as inertia, making us feel stuck despite our intentions.

When left unchecked, Dormant Power can lead to a way of living I refer to as the **Unintended Life.** This is a state of unconscious navigation, where instead of steering toward our true passions and purpose, we drift along the currents of external demands and societal expectations. It's not about a lack of effort or laziness, but a deeper disconnection from our own agency and intentionality.

Inaction Exercise

We can examine more closely our motives behind our inaction by asking ourselves some basic questions. Reflect and write down your answers to these questions:

- What feels intimidating about pursuing success in this particular area?
- Why am I avoiding taking action toward this goal?
- What is holding me back from pushing through this and reaching my full potential?

By questioning our inaction and challenging our fears, we reclaim our power to create the life we truly want. The choice is always ours.

The Cost of Arrogance: A Miscalculation that Clouds our Perception

The mistake I'm referring to is arrogance, an inflated sense of self that can distort how we see ourselves and our circumstances. It's a faulty belief that we can predict the future, which often prevents us from taking risks and pursuing our dreams. When we convince ourselves that we already know the outcome of a situation, why bother trying? This isn't a rational thought but a fear disguised as certainty. By buying into these illusions, we hinder ourselves from chasing what we truly desire, actively sabotaging our dreams and stifling our ambitions before they even have a chance to flourish.

The Miscalculation of Arrogance:

This inner resistance to change is often rooted in four common obstacles I've identified:

1. **Arrogance** or resistance to change, the belief that we already know the outcome.
2. **Fear** of change, a protective instinct that keeps us in stuck in our comfort zone.
3. **Limiting beliefs**, the self-imposed rules we create about what's possible for us.
4. **A failure of imagination**, the inability to envision a future different from our present.

Recognizing which of these holds you back is the first step toward moving forward. The path begins with honesty. By facing these miscalculations, we stop sabotaging our journey. The choice is simple: remain trapped in certainty, or step into the unknown and begin creating the life you desire. The next step is to choose to see with new eyes.

Figure 12.3: Arrogance is the illusion of a crown, built on a fragile foundation that will inevitably shatter.

Figure 12.3: A stark silhouette stands upright with an upturned head, embodying arrogance's self-importance and detachment. At its feet, a shattered mirror reflects fractured self-image through distorted faces in the shards, while radiating pieces reflecting fractured relationships. Above, a crown drips black liquid, symbolizing corrupted power and moral decay in a fragile façade masking unstable reality.

Reflective question:
When you look at the fragmented mirror of your own life, what fears or certainties are you willing to release to see a truer reflection?

Personal reflections:
What if…

> …your self-perceptions are outdated?

> …your current path isn't your best option?

> …what you believe you are able to accomplish is only half the truth?

> …it is time to re-examine your beliefs?

Chapter Summary: Transformation begins by confronting self-rejection and the prison of entrenched beliefs. Growth springs from resilience, the choice to rise instead of being defined by setbacks. As beliefs shape reality, questioning them opens the door to liberation. Awareness of limiting narratives reminds us that our words can bind or free us. When we challenge inner barriers, dormant power converts to purposeful motion. Yet progress stalls when certainty turns to arrogance, trapping us in fear and self-sabotage. Choosing intention demands courage, to trust our inner guidance and move boldly into the unknown.

At the edge of certainty, we meet the illusion of Dormant Power. Confronting this resistance clarifies the structures that keep us bound. To see differently, we must listen to the rhythm of our own unrest:

The Miscalculation of Certainty

The self-rejecting seed is turned to light,

But shadows bloom where future meets the fight.

Beware the viral limitation's hold,

A binding fear on hearts we've left untold.

To guard the comfort we still call our home,

We weave the lie that keeps us where we roam.

We feel the drag of dormant power's chain

And walk the paths that promise empty gain.

The engine hums, its purpose left untaught,

So still we dwell in lives we never sought.

This stillness hides a fear in polished guise,

A flawed equation shimmering behind the eyes.

We wear the certainty of failure's end,

The quiet arrogance that will not bend.

"Why move ahead? The outcome is defined",

Thus speaks the saboteur within the mind.

Now shatter every mirror's fractured view;

The cost of comfort is the life concealed from you.

Only forward motion breaks the spell;

Uncrown the fear and trust the tale you tell.

See with new eyes, ignite the daring start;

Unbind the weight that stills your waiting heart.

Chapter XIII: The Still Point Current: Foundational Habits for Inner Peace

Figure 13.1: Starve Negativity - Break free from the tangle of negative thoughts by stepping into light and engaging in what nurtures well-being.

The following are some effective coping strategies to help you manage negativity and improve your overall well-being:

Starve Negativity
We can starve negativity by redirecting our attention to something productive or enjoyable, and by avoiding the trap of obsessing over what's bothering us. Keeping busy and getting out of the house helps break the cycle of negative thoughts, making it easier to regain a sense of balance.

Foundational Habits:

Animal Friendships
Spending time with animals can be particularly healing. Their energy is pure, authentic and their intentions are transparent, offering us acceptance without judgment or criticism. Animals can also teach us the subtle aspects of transmuting energy, reminding us of ways to break free from the continuous cycle of being stuck in our thoughts.

Dietary Adjustments
If your diet is filled with highly processed, sugary foods and lacks sufficient fruits, vegetables, fiber, and protein, it might be contributing to mood swings, inflammation, and insulin spikes. These foods often create addictive cycles, making you crave more as you consume them. Instead, choose whole, unprocessed options: proteins, fruits, vegetables, proteins, along with low-glycemic foods. These choices support not only physical health but also your mood and overall well-being.

Tree Networking
Tree Networking: is a term I coined to describe the practice of immersing oneself in nature, especially among the healing energy of trees, in order to disconnect from daily stressors and electronic devices while allowing the soothing environment to rejuvenate the mind and body. Whether basking in the sun beneath their branches or breathing fresh air in their presence, trees and the natural world have a soothing effect on our bodies, helping us to recharge our energy and restore balance. When engaging in Tree Networking, turn off your phone or leave it behind to truly disconnect from distractions and ground with the earth.

Practice Unconditional Self-Compassion
Practicing unconditional self-compassion is most essential. When we embrace ourselves fully, negativity has less room to take up space in our lives (see the Superimposition Principle). Cultivating self-compassion creates an immediate improvement in our outlook, on life and, makes us energetically more appealing to ourselves and others.

Use this exercise when you are feeling overwhelmed.

The Anchor Exercise
Set a timer for 10 min.
Sit comfortably in a chair and close your eyes.
Bring your attention to your breath.
Observe the feeling of the chair supporting your back and legs.
Notice the physical sensation of your feet making contact with the ground.
Imagine heavy anchors attached to your feet and pulling your energy down through your legs and into the earth.
Notice any areas where you feel tension in your body.
Imagine the weight of those anchors pulling that tension down through your body, down your legs, and into the earth.
Take slow deliberate inhalations through the nose and then out through the nose.
Visualize your tension releasing throughout.
Continue until you feel things begin to release.

Chapter Summary: This chapter offers practical guidance for weathering life's challenges without allowing negativity to harden the heart. It emphasizes maintaining faith while gently redirecting the mind from obsessive thoughts, cultivating supportive habits, and finding comfort in animal companionship and nourishing food. The chapter introduces two restorative practices: the Anchor Exercise, a visualization for releasing worry and tension, and Tree Networking, an invitation to reconnect with nature and restore inner harmony. It closes with a reminder that unconditional self-compassion is the anchor of true self connection, an energy that uplifts perspective and strengthens our connection with others.

Reflective question
When you catch your own reflection unexpectedly, what's the very first feeling that surfaces before your mind has a chance to intervene?

The Still Point Current

The world outside may spin too fast,

While shadows of the past can cast

A net of worry on the mind,

Where quiet peace is hard to find.

Yet we possess the tools to shift,

A quiet refuge, a true gift.

We choose the focus of our sight,

Starve darkness by feeding light.

We seek the pure, authentic friend,

Whose open gaze holds no pretense,

The loving animal, spirit bright,

Reflecting calm, accepting light.

Then journey to the ancient wood,

Where roots run deep and understood.

Connect with all the silent, tall,

And hear the steady current call.

We lift the eraser, smooth and wide,

And clear the anxious thoughts inside,

A spacious calm where balance breathes,

An inner compass for our needs.

For peace within is not a whim,

But practice born of conscious shift.

Through quiet strength, awake and strong,

We find the place where we belong.

Chapter XIV: The Ripple's Voice: Language, Presence, and Energetic Influence

Figure 14.1: A visual expression of **Word Transference**, where spoken language crystallizes into lived reality.

The Ripple's Voice: Language, Presence, and Energetic Influence

The Energetic Resonance Effect (E.R.E.) is the practice of broadcasting our energy inward and outward. This energetic broadcast can be beneficial not only for ourselves but also for others we interact with. If you could see this broadcast, it would look like a ripple of fine mist radiating outward from the person activating it, like the expanding waves created by a stone tossed into a still pond. I call this **Energetic Waves**, a name for how our feelings and intentions radiate beyond us.

This invisible ripple of uplifting energy emanates, creating a sympathetic resonance that enhances the emotional and spiritual well-being of both the person practicing it as well as those around us. The ripple flows infinitely outward, carried by intention and feeling, unimpeded by any material. It's not a physical wave but a wave of consciousness, traveling to the farthest corners of the universe to connect with others on a more enhanced level.

In stark contrast, negative energy feels dense and heavy, like a weight we carry within. It settles in the body much like a damp towel, pressing down and making us sluggish and weighed down. Unlike more obvious emotions, this heaviness doesn't easily broadcast outward. When left unresolved, this stagnant emotional state can drain vitality and negatively impact overall health.

The Power of Influence

One remarkable aspect of practicing E.R.E. is the way a single individual can catalyze a transformative shift within a group's energetic field. Through focused intention, one's bioenergetic field can harmonize and elevate the collective atmosphere, guiding others toward greater coherence and optimism. This demonstrates the capacity each of us holds to shape not only our personal energy but also the shared resonance of those around us. I refer to this phenomenon as **Energetic Influence**. (For more on this topic, see Chapter 19: The Prism Threshold.)

Reflective question:

When have you felt your personal energy or mood influence the atmosphere of a room or group, either positively or negatively, and what did that experience teach you about your own "Energetic Influence"?

The Ignition Points: Language and Presence
The Power of Language

A powerful way to expand our energy is through the **words we choose**. We can use certain words as tools to change our internal state. The feeling we cultivate on the inside is what radiates outward through the E.R.E.

One of my go-to words for this transmutation I previously mentioned is optimism. I define optimism as a forward-looking mindset that sees possibilities and expects a favorable outcome, regardless of external circumstances. Accessing its qualities immediately improves how I feel internally. This energy helps me increase and amplify my transmutational abilities.

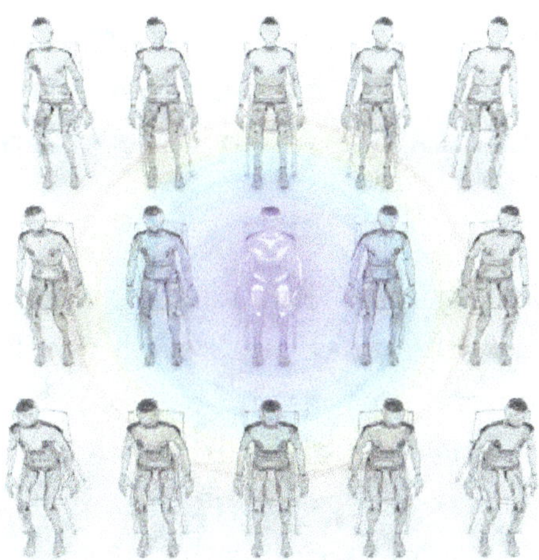

Figure 14.2: illustrates **Energetic Influence** as uplifting waves radiating outward from a single individual.

Another powerful word for energetic work I previously discussed is authenticity. I define authenticity as the expression of one's truest self, projected outward without self-judgment or pretense. It strengthens my connection to myself and allows me to radiate my true being, making the E.R.E. even more potent.

Our words travel through our body, mind, and spirit, touching the way we feel, think, and come to know ourselves as well as our interactions with others. Words are more than sounds; they hold energy that molds both inner experience and outer life. This process, I call **Word Transference**, acknowledges how language shapes our outcomes. A word can seal a promise, ignite inspiration, or trigger unexpected emotional consequences. This concept calls on us to recognize this creative power, cautioning that careless language can forge negative outcomes, beliefs and self-perceptions.

Each spoken word carries its own vibrational signature. Positive speech imprints uplifting energy on the mind and body, helping us embody those qualities. Negative speech, by contrast, binds harmful energy to us, affecting our mindset, health, self-worth, prosperity, and relationships.

Sometimes, the most powerful communication doesn't involve words at all. It happens in the quiet moments between people when your presence becomes the message. I refer to this as **Intentional Presence**. It's not just about being silent; it's an active and deliberate choice to be fully attentive.

Think about a time when you felt completely content and at peace with your life. That calm, positive energy radiates from you, and others can feel it, causing them to relax and feel more uplifted. This kind of intentionality is a way of communicating your state without speaking a word.

It's easy to mistake this for other kinds of quiet. Such as an awkward silence often feels empty, a vacuum waiting to be filled with something needing to be said. The cold silence of anger or resentment can feel heavy and suffocating to all in the vicinity. Intentional Presence, however, is vibrant. It's a silence full of genuine attention, compassion, and sincerity. This difference in energy allows others to feel the sincerity behind your quietness, making it a powerful tool for connection rather than a source of discomfort. This state of contentment is a potent blend of optimism and authenticity. In this state, words don't need to be expressed; the energy speaks for itself.

Reflective Question:
When was the last time you felt a genuine, positive connection with someone through Intentional Presence, and how did that unspoken energy feel?

The Ultimate Flashpoint and Application
Authenticity is the foundation of transmutation. It's about not creating judgments about oneself or others, which makes it potent in its own right. Optimism is a dynamic offshoot of authenticity; it's exciting but more grounded. Beyond even this potent energy lies the true pinnacle of transmutation: **exuberance**.

Exuberance is potent, powerful, invigorating, and at times intoxicating energetic word. When you work with this word's energy, it creates a powerful, exquisite vibration that radiates from our chest, effortlessly generating excitement and a sense of potency. Think of the pure joy you feel when you complete a long-term goal or start a passion project you've been dreaming about, that's the energy of exuberance.

Application & Troubleshooting

Using the principles of the E.R.E., we transmute and attach excitement to the frequency and phase of "exuberance." However because "exuberance" by nature is already an exciting word, the attachment activates the second you tap into its frequency, requiring less focus to get things started.

If you're having difficulty transmuting and attaching the E.R.E. principles, it's most often due to external or mental distractions. Ask yourself: Am I calm or harried? Am I in the present, or am I stressing about other tasks?

To access this power, you must become fully present, grounded in the right-now moment. Disconnect from everything else, if even only for a brief while. Once you begin to "feel" that spark, you'll know you've accessed it. This process creates a blueprint, teaching your body what it feels like to tap into this powerful words energy. As you continue to practice, activating this feeling it can become second nature, and the E.R.E. will become a natural extension of your being.

To help get yourself in the right state of mind, try listening to music, taking a walk, playing a sport, engaging in a hobby, or sitting quietly for a short while. Find an activity that helps you feel more connected to your true source.

A Word of Caution: Recognizing Stagnation

Trying to force a shift in energy when you're feeling down can be counterproductive. The E.R.E. works best when your energy is centered, not emotionally overwhelmed. Forcing a shift when you're emotionally overwhelmed is like trying to stop a speeding freight train, it's a recipe for what I call **Energetic Derailment**. Instead, we distract ourselves and allow that momentum to gradually slow through distractions. By letting this counterproductive energy dissipate, we can then more effectively shift our mindset without any derailment.

When Energy Goes Flat

As you become more aware of your energetic presence, you may begin to notice that some people routinely exhibit flattened empty energy. It may even appear squashed or nonexistent. I refer to this as being **Energetically Detached**.

Being Energetically Detached describes someone who appears emotionally muted and closed-off. This hidden tension erodes optimism by fostering negativity, withdrawal, and a sense of powerless disconnection from our true potential and the possibilities that exist.

Energetic Detachment may indicate:
- Disconnecting emotionally from our own feelings.
- Not able to see the good in situations.
- Lacking self-compassion.
- Engaging in excessive self-criticism.
- Overly critical of others.

Your energy speaks for you. It communicates your inner truth, mindset, and capacity for self-compassion. When we disconnect from this authentic energy, we experience Energetic Detachment, the opposite of engaging with our true selves. Recognizing this disconnection is a powerful step toward consciously cultivating the power that resides within us.

Authenticity Exercise - Reflect on these questions:
- What aspects of expressing my authenticity feels most uncomfortable, and what am I afraid will happen if I push through that discomfort?

- If I embraced my true self, how would that feel internally and how might it appear to others?

- What changes could I make right now to become more aligned with my authentic self?

~ Our mindset holds the key which unlocks the door to boundless optimism.

Chapter Summary: This chapter explores how our inner energy projects outward through feelings, intentions, and language. It highlights two key points for energetic growth: Intentional Presence, the calm expression of a centered state, and the creative Power of Language through Word Transference, where words carry energetic blueprints shaping reality. Positive language supports well-being and relationships, while negativity binds harmful energy. Tools like optimism, authenticity, and exuberance fuel energetic transformation. It warns against forced change when overwhelmed and defines Energetic Detachment as inauthentic. It encourages cultivating presence and mindful speech as essential for manifesting desired realities.

Reflective question:
What is the energetic blueprint of the words you use most often?

The work of transformation is never silent; it radiates outward, touching everything it encounters. This poem encapsulates how your internal energy becomes a force in the world.

The Conscious Current

The stream of success begins within,

A hidden current where our choices win.

It draws in moments or pushes them away;

Pause and ask: what moves inside today?

The ripple starts in quiet core,

Expanding outward evermore.

Like stone in water, feeling spreads,

A conscious wave that never ends.

Heavy energy moves slow and dim,

A stagnant pool where light grows thin.

But clear intent can shift the air,

Turning tides toward what is fair.

Your presence ignites the living field,

Words hold blueprints you unconsciously wield.

Choose optimism, see possibilities bright,

Or truth, alive in accessible light.

Even silence speaks, resonant, whole,

Not empty hush, but mindful control.

Presence blooms to be a guiding glow,

Revealing all we inwardly know.

The ultimate spark, exuberant and pure,

Is joy that rises, knowing it will endure.

To touch this current, be here, awake;

Let the past dissolve, let worry break.

Don't force the shift when weary or torn;

Let motion rest, like a softened storm.

Return renewed, with tender care,

To your authentic self, bright and aware.

Your energy tells the story true,

The conscious light you are meant to share,

Chapter XV: The Ignition Threshold: Neuroplasticity and Neural Repair

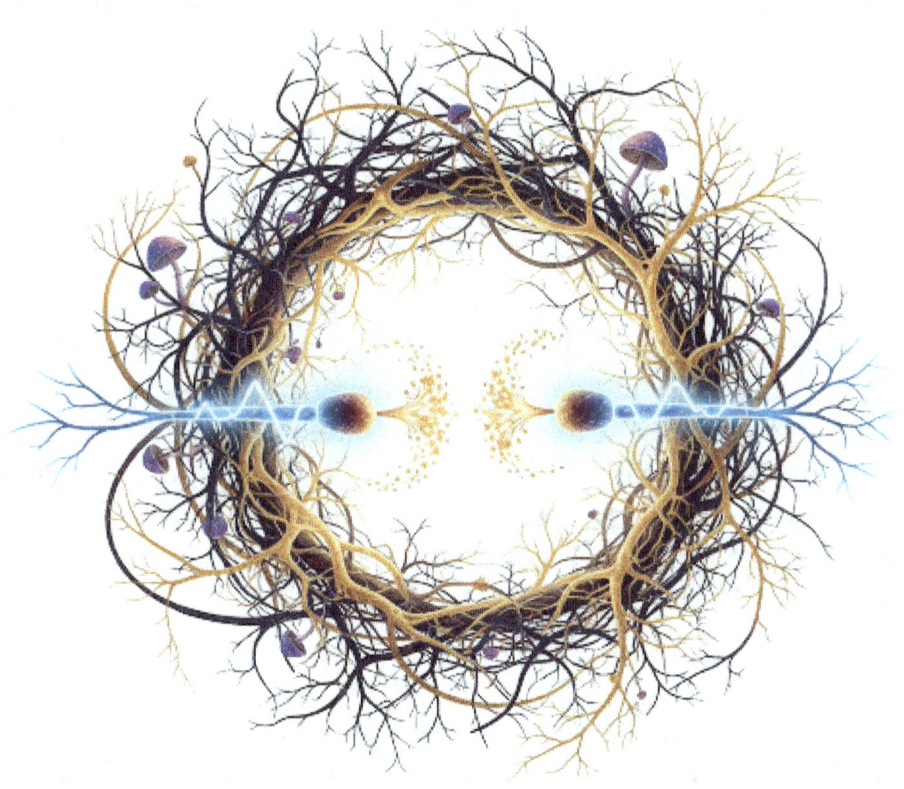

Figure 15.1: A visual exploration of **Synaptic Firing, and Neuroplasticity.**

Figure 15.1: A wreath of intertwined branches and roots in brown and golden tones symbolizes vitality. Small purple and red mushrooms dot the branches. Two luminous beams, cut through the center, flowing through the branches. This image evokes mystical energy in an organic circuit, reflecting synaptic firing and neuroplasticity, highlighting its role in healing brain connectivity and transformation.

Synaptic firing is the way brain cells, and neurons communicate with one another. Think of it as a conversation happening in the brain. When a neuron wants to send a message, it generates an electrical impulse, called an action potential, that travels down its length. When this signal reaches the end, it crosses a small gap, called a synapse, to reach the next cell. The second cell receives the message and passes the information along, creating a chain reaction. This exchange of impulses is what enables every thought, movement, and sensation.

Building on this foundation, we can better understand the therapeutic and healing potential of psilocybin, a compound found in Psilocybe cubensis mushrooms (often called magic mushrooms). Psilocybin, long recognized for its psychotropic effects, has also been shown to encourage healing and neuroplasticity, the brain's ability to reorganize and form new connections. This capacity to "rewire" neural pathways may offer a pathway to healing in conditions such as depression, where those pathways have become disrupted.

My own healing journey provides a living example of this possibility. It has been nonlinear, full of twists and turns I never could have predicted, and one pivotal source of growth came from where I least expected. For a long time, I hesitated to share this part of my story, fearing it might be misunderstood. Yet leaving it out would mean omitting a vital part of this healing journey. During my deeper explorations into the Energetic Resonance Effect, I felt an undeniable pull toward exploring the healing potential of magic mushrooms. In time, I came to realize these were not separate inquiries at all, but two facets of the same unfolding, each amplifying the other and carrying me toward more breakthrough.

Psilocybin and Neural Repair

Research shows psilocybin has been shown to help repair neural pathways disrupted by neurological conditions such as depression. Depression can impair the brain's ability to function optimally, but psilocybin has demonstrated a powerful potential to facilitate healing in the affected areas. Unlike traditional antidepressants requiring long-term use, psilocybin's effects can be rapid and transformative. After exploring its benefits through experimentation, I found the results remarkable. I believe this mushroom-derived compound holds the key to the future of brain health and repair, potentially offering a safer, more effective alternative to prescription antidepressant medications.

A Path to Wisdom

Additionally, psilocybin experiences can expand perception, allowing individuals to perceive connections and concepts previously unnoticed. Many report an increased sense of connectedness and greater understanding of themselves and their world. This shift in perspective is a key part of psilocybin's story as a source of insight.

Scientific Insights

A study from University College London and Imperial College London analyzed fMRI brain scans of nearly 60 people with depression, finding that psilocybin reduced connections within overactive brain regions involved in rumination, such as the so called Default Mode Network (DMN), salience, and executive networks. At the same time, it increased connectivity with previously less-integrated regions. This neural rewiring helps individuals break free from rigid thought patterns, lowers emotional avoidance, and improves cognitive function. These brain changes correlated with reductions in depressive symptoms lasting often long term and were not seen in those receiving antidepressants and SSRI's, suggesting psilocybin acts differently than antidepressants (Kurtzman, 2022).

Neuroplasticity and Mechanisms

Psilocybin and other serotonergic psychedelics target 5-HT2A receptors abundant in brain networks that become overactive in depression. The prevailing hypothesis is that these drugs disrupt dysfunctional networks, allowing them to reorganize in more adaptive ways during the following days and weeks (Kurtzman, 2022).

A five-year follow-up study of 24 patients with severe depression found that a single psilocybin dose produced sustained improvement for 67% of participants, along with reduced anxiety and improved daily functioning.

Self-Discovery Through Psilocybin and Meditation

Both the practice of meditation and psilocybin use can accelerate a journey toward authenticity through complementary means. Meditation cultivates present-moment awareness, enabling the observation of thoughts without attachment. Psilocybin encourages shifts in perception while supporting the repair and creation of neural pathways. Though distinct in method, together they can work synergistically toward greater alignment with one's authentic self.

Dosage Considerations

Psilocybin can function as an internal reset, reconnecting us to presence. Micro-dosing, typically reported between ~0.1–0.3 grams of dried mushrooms, brings subtle, uplifting effects without inducing a full psychedelic trip. Smaller doses are believed to be very conducive for facilitating brain repair. These small amounts often work beneath the threshold of conscious perception, where neural recalibration and pathway repair can occur. In contrast, macrodosing (1 gram or more dried) initiates a more immersive and sustained psychedelic experience. It is important to note that potency varies by individual sensitivity and also by the specific type of magic mushroom, as different strains contain varying levels of active compounds that influence the overall effects.

Creativity and The Neuroplastic Muse

Psilocybin has been linked to enhanced creativity by reducing activity in the brain's Default Mode Network, the internal editor that suppresses novel or unusual ideas (Carhart-Harris et al., 2012). A reduction in DMN activity opens the mind to new connections and perspectives, facilitating healing and neuroplasticity.

Personal Healing and the Energetic Resonance Effect

In my healing journey, a modest psilocybin dose improved my outlook. It also enhanced my ability to practice the Energetic Resonance Effect more effectively, making me a more effective transmuter. These benefits highlighted psilocybin's powerful role in transformation.

The Monster in the Room: Big Pharma

The pharmaceutical industry's immense financial interests influence Western medicine's slow and cautious stance on alternative therapies like psychedelics. This sector has historically generated doubt, fear, and stigma around treatments outside its control, relying on lifelong customers rather than cures for conditions.

The Problems with Antidepressants

Prescription antidepressants carry a range of potential risks and side effects. One notable concern is discontinuation syndrome, in which stopping certain antidepressants can lead to extensive withdrawal symptoms that complicate tapering without professional guidance. Although distinct from addiction, this syndrome can present significant challenges requiring careful management. In rare cases, particularly with high doses or drug combinations, excess serotonin may accumulate, leading to serotonin syndrome, a potentially dangerous condition demanding urgent medical care.

Certain types of antidepressants, especially monoamine oxidase inhibitors (MAOIs), impose strict dietary and medication restrictions due to the risk of severe interactions.

Long-term use of some antidepressants has also been linked to hyponatremia, a condition of abnormally low sodium levels in the blood. Additionally, some studies suggest that extended use may raise the risk of metabolic disorders such as diabetes and may be associated with cognitive decline over time.

Symptom Management vs. Root Cause Healing
Modern healthcare often excels at managing symptoms, but true wellness arises from addressing the root causes that generate those symptoms. Treating underlying causes rather than merely suppressing symptoms offers significant advantages. Healing restores the body's natural functions and vitality, allowing people to experience genuine wellness rather than just alleviating discomfort. Addressing root causes prevents disease progression that could worsen if only symptoms are treated. Compared to symptom management, which often relies on medications with their own side effects, root cause healing works in harmony with the body's natural processes, minimizing adverse reactions.

Healing enables long-term resolution, freeing individuals from the need for ongoing symptom management and lifelong medication use. While healing might require an upfront investment, it can be cost-effective by eliminating recurring expenses such as repeat prescriptions, frequent doctor visits, or treatments for complications. Furthermore, understanding what caused the condition provides empowerment and tools for maintaining health, preventing future recurrences. Holistic healing tends to improve multiple aspects of health simultaneously, as many systems in the body are interconnected.

Reflective Question:
What personal beliefs or societal norms have you accepted without question, and what tools might you use to explore them more thoroughly?

Disclaimer and Limitation of Liability
The information in this book, particularly regarding the exploration of altered states and the discussion of psychoactive substances, is provided solely for educational and intellectual purposes. It does not constitute medical advice, psychological counseling, diagnosis, or treatment. The approaches described are experimental in nature and based on energetic and theoretical frameworks.

The author and publisher make no guarantee of any specific outcome or result from applying the principles or methods discussed. Readers should exercise personal discretion and comply with all applicable laws and safety guidelines; this book does not endorse or promote illegal activity, and the legality of these substances varies widely by jurisdiction.

Do not use psilocybin or any psychoactive substances while driving, operating machinery, or performing work-related duties. The reader assumes all risk and responsibility for the use, misuse, or interpretation of the information contained herein. The author and publisher disclaim all liability for any injury, loss, or damage arising from the application or misuse of information presented in this material.

This list of contraindications is not exhaustive or all-inclusive. The science and regulations around these topics are constantly evolving.

It is the sole responsibility of the reader to consult with a qualified healthcare professional, physician, or psychiatrist before making any changes to their medication, health regimen, or considering the use of any psychoactive substances, legal or otherwise.

The author and publisher assume no liability for any adverse effects or consequences resulting from the use of any suggestions, procedures, or discussions presented in this material.

Specific Contraindications and Risk Factors

Individuals with the following conditions or circumstances should **not** consider the use of certain psychoactive substances (such as psilocybin) discussed in this book, due to potentially severe and unpredictable negative health consequences:

APPENDIX A: Medical Contraindications and Warnings:

Important Note: The following list of medical contraindications and warnings is provided for informational purposes only. This list is not comprehensive, and it does not substitute for the advice, diagnosis, or treatment of a qualified medical professional. Individuals should consult their physician before engaging in any practice described in this book.

Appendix A: Contraindications for Psilocybin Use

Category	Specific Contraindication	Rationale (Risk/ Mechanism)
Psychiatric Conditions	Primary Psychotic Disorders (e.g., Schizophrenia, Schizoaffective Disorder)	Risk of precipitating or worsening psychosis.

Psychiatric Conditions	Bipolar I Disorder	Heightened risk of inducing a manic episode.
Psychiatric Conditions	First-Degree Family History of Psychotic Disorders	Exclusion criterion in trials due to inherited risk of psychosis.
Psychiatric Conditions	Significant Trauma History without Stabilization	Risk of overwhelming emotional dysregulation or suicidal due to lack of coping skills.
Psychiatric Conditions	Previous Adverse Reaction to Psychedelics	History of prolonged psychosis or suicidal ideation after prior use.
Cardiovascular Conditions	Uncontrolled Hypertension (High Blood Pressure)	Risk of cardiac events (e.g., heart attack, stroke) due to elevated blood pressure.
Drug-Drug Interactions	Serotonergic Medications (SSRIs, SNRIs, MAOIs, TCAs, Triptans)	Risk of a potentially life-threatening condition called Serotonin Syndrome. Can also blunt the psilocybin effect.
Drug-Drug Interactions	Stimulant Drugs (e.g., amphetamines, cocaine)	Increased risk of severe heart rate and blood pressure elevation.
Drug-Drug Interactions	Antipsychotics	May significantly blunt or eliminate the psychedelic effects by blocking serotonin receptors.
Other Conditions	Pregnancy and Breast-feeding	Insufficient reliable safety data; avoidance is recommended.

Other Conditions	Epilepsy/Seizure Disorder	Potential for increased risk of seizures.

Chapter Summary: This chapter explores synaptic firing and how psilocybin supports healing disrupted neural pathways in depression, highlighting scientific evidence of enhanced neuroplasticity and lasting symptom relief. It integrates the author's personal healing experience and the Energetic Resonance Effect, contrasts psilocybin's root-cause healing with conventional antidepressants, and addresses safe dosing, creative potential, medical screening, and institutional resistance to psychedelics. The chapter concludes by positioning psilocybin as a powerful, optional tool within broader energetic and psychological transformation.

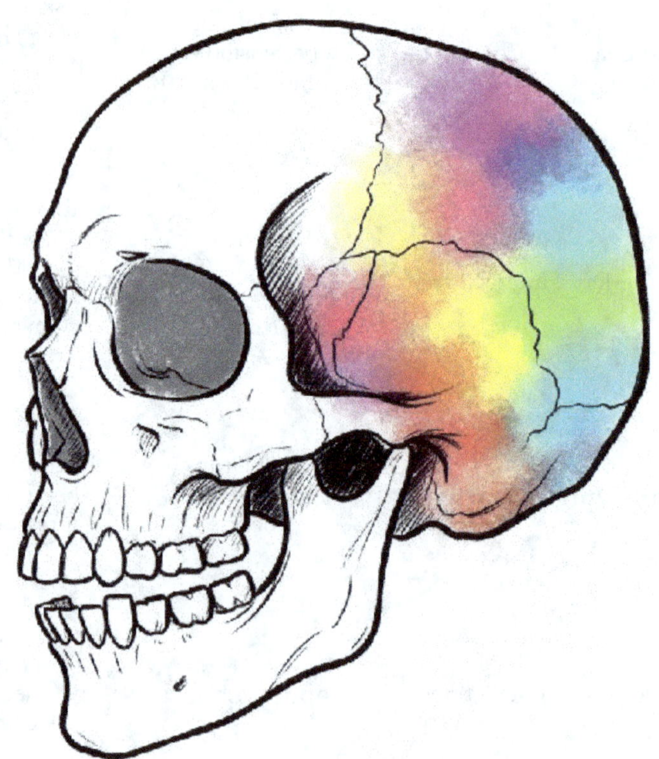

Figure 15.2: Crossing the Rubicon - The mind's rewired pathways after Psilocybe Cubensis.

The ultimate catalyst for transformation is often found where we least expect it. This poem reflects the, almost mystical rebirth possible when we cross the threshold of inner change.

Pure Magic

These mushrooms are no meal,

a dish for the mind, not the mouth.

They are metamorphosis,

a spell disguised as flesh.

They unlock hidden doors,

whispering secrets of change,

transforming what was lost,

a self reborn,

ancient yet anew.

One taste rekindles forgotten fire,

igniting unseen worlds

for those who dare to see.

So tell me,

will you drink the mystery?

Will you cross the threshold

into realms concealed,

shadowed yet familiar,

where life wears the mask of magic?

Figure 15.3: Wild-magic - A wild magic mushroom patch.

Chapter XVI: The Whisper in the Wave: Unlocking the Enhanced Frisson Effect

Figure 16.1: A visual representation of **the Enhanced Frisson Effect**.

Figure 16.1: The Enhanced Frisson Effect: translucent human torso and head glows centered by a radiant golden-yellow heart symbolizing emotional-spiritual core. Electric colorful tendrils wave outward, evoking Enhanced Frisson from music. Dark veins trace the form, transforming sensory input into energy, with palm waves suggesting emission or reception of transformative sound waves.

Unlocking the Enhanced Frisson Effect

I long struggled to articulate a powerful sensation that overtook me whenever certain types of music played. I drafted and deleted countless attempts at explanation until, by chance, I encountered someone describing the very experience I had been trying to put into words -Frisson.

Frisson: The Physical Response to Music

The phenomenon known as frisson, a physical and emotional response to music, often arising during climactic passages such as a key change, a sudden vocal entry, or the introduction of a new instrument (Sachs et al., 2016). It manifests as shivers, goosebumps, or hair standing on end, accompanied by a rush of excitement and emotional intensity. Research shows that people who are especially receptive to new experiences and emotionally sensitive to art are more likely to experience frisson (Nusbaum & Silvia, 2011). These individuals tend to score higher on "openness to experience," one of the Big Five personality traits associated with curiosity, creativity, and a deep appreciation for beauty (Colver & El-Alayli, 2016).

The Enhanced Frisson Effect

As my skill in utilizing the E.R.E. developed, I discovered a compelling phenomenon which I call the **Enhanced Frisson Effect,** a transmutation of musical sound frequencies through deliberate energetic interaction. When listening to certain artists, especially those producing wordless, instrumental tracks, I experienced sensations far more intense than traditional frisson: euphoric, climactic, and fully embodied, as if the music's energy radiated through me.

What intrigued me most was that these sensations arose not from the dominant melodies but from the subtle, almost imperceptible sounds carefully woven into the background of the music, the delicate tonal textures and harmonic layers that many listeners might overlook. Within these nuanced gradations, the music seemed to come alive with an organic vitality that resonated with my own energetic field, amplifying the frisson response to euphoric levels.

Crucially, this Enhanced Frisson Effect rarely emerged from songs with vocals or lyrics. Instead, it requires purely instrumental soundscapes, allowing the subtle tonal and harmonic elements to interact with the listener's energetic field. Vocals often anchor perception to language and narrative, which can interrupt the delicate energetic resonance necessary for this heightened neuroenergetic activation. It is within these abstract, non-verbal sonic environments that the transmutation of sound frequencies through energetic interaction manifests most powerfully.

These experiences did not arise from any chemical influence but from a resonance between music and energetic transmutation of the music, the direct interplay of sound vibration and the principles of the E.R.E. I came to recognize this intensified frisson as the convergence of the natural frisson response transmuted with the Energetic Resonance Effect, producing a surge of heightened neuroenergetic activity and an expanded state of pleasure, what I term the **Enhanced Frisson Effect**. This phenomenon suggests that the transmutation of musical frequencies through the E.R.E. can amplify inner sensation and open consciousness to powerfully transformative states.

Chapter Summary: This chapter explores frisson, the goosebumps from emotionally charged music, common in those open to experience, and the Enhanced Frisson Effect (E.F.E.), fusing it with the Energetic Resonance Effect (E.R.E.) for euphoric, full-body neuro- energetic highs. Triggered by instrumental soundscapes in conjunction with transmuting the E.R.E. which engages with subtle tonal textures and harmonics, bypassing lyrics for direct sonic immersion. This conscious interaction amplifies inner sensation, expands consciousness, and awakens emotional transformation.

While the science of frisson explains the physical reaction, and the E.R.E. explains the energetic mechanics, the experience itself often defies technical description. To truly understand the shift from a simple shiver to a full energetic expansion, we must look beyond definitions. The following lines capture the essence of this transmutation:

The Resonance Transmuted

I used to chase a name for the shivering,

A word for the ghost that brushed my skin,

When the key would shift, or the strings begin,

And the goosebumps rose like a tide rolling in.

They called it Frisson, the open heart's prize,

Where hair stands high and the spirit flies.

But I found a depth where the shiver reforms,

Beyond the biology, rewriting norms.

Through practice and presence, a new gate revealed,

Where sound waves dance with the energy field.

No chemical spark, no substance required,

Just the current where soul and the nerve are wired.

The voices quiet, the lyrics recede,

Words are but anchors the mind doesn't need.

Give me the texture, the instrumental sway,

Where the subtle vibrations come out to play.

Not the dominant beat, but the layers beneath,

The hidden harmonics that quietly breathe.

They flow through the being, euphoric, bright,

A transmutation of sound into light.

Organic vitality, resonant, pure,

Where self and the music merge and blur.

In the wordless expansion, the energy speaks,

The Enhanced Frisson, the language it seeks.

Chapter XVII: The Variables Lab: Shifting Your Trajectory

Figure 17.1: The Variables Lab: Shifting perspectives and releasing limiting beliefs, we create the inner order needed to welcome new possibilities.

Figure 17.1: Dark, thorny vines trap shadowed figures amid cracked stone and a shriveled apple on the left, symbolizing scarcity. A glowing central portal bridges to the right, where a vibrant apple tree laden with luminous fruit surrounds joyful figures, butterflies, and a radiant path, embodying abundance. The composition shifts from darkness and constriction to light, openness, and collaborative flow

The Variables Lab: Shifting Your Trajectory

When we convince ourselves that a situation is bound to unfold in a less-than-desirable way, we often unintentionally create internal resistance that distorts our perceptions of what is possible. In doing so, we block potential opportunities from reaching us. However, with just a small shift in perspective, we can loosen the grip of limiting expectations and open ourselves to more fruitful possibilities. This fundamental concept is described by what I call the **Trajectory Equation**, which posits that a person's current life direction (T), combined with their limiting or expanding beliefs (B), interacts with and can influence the likelihood of a resulting outcome (O). Therefore, by deliberately altering the belief component (B), we might potentially initiate a measurable shift to a more favorable outcome.

Viewing experience through a lens of scarcity, where resources, opportunities, and success are seen as finite, often proves counterproductive to personal growth. This mindset, which interprets the world as a zero-sum game, frequently manifests in professional settings as a constant need to one-up colleagues in the workplace. Rather than fostering collaboration, it encourages unnecessary competition, leading people to hoard information and position themselves against others for a perceived limited number of promotions or recognition. This same scarcity mindset can infiltrate personal relationships, eroding trust as people grow wary of others "taking" their share of happiness or success. In daily life, whether interacting with the public or with companies, this belief system can foster a state of perpetual defensiveness and the feeling of always struggling over scarce resources. Ultimately, this approach prevents people from recognizing and capitalizing on the abundance of possibilities that exist, both for themselves and for others.

The power of this shift lies in understanding that even small adjustments to our beliefs begin to influence how we experience and respond to unfolding events. The process starts by examining your current expectations. What are you already assuming will happen? Once identified, introduce a new internal narrative such as: "I don't know how this situation will unfold, but I will remain open and hopeful for the best possible outcome." Then begin to imagine your preferred outcome as already in motion.

At the same time, release any attachments to negative expectations that don't serve you. The more we ruminate on negative outcomes, the more we reinforce them as greater possibilities. If fears resurface, practice mindful redirection by shifting your focus elsewhere.

To better understand how this works, imagine a circle with many arrows radiating outward, each arrow representing a possible trajectory or probability for an event that has yet to occur. Since we cannot predict the future with certainty, fixating on one expected result, especially a negative one, limits our openness to alternatives. Beneficial outcomes often arise beyond what we can presently conceive, revealing that possibility itself expands when we release the need to control the unknown.

The many arrows represent the unlimited possible outcomes that could unfold. The **red** arrow symbolizes a high-probability but less desirable scenario, one you've imagined and begun to expect. In contrast, the **green** arrow represents a less likely yet much more desirable possibility.

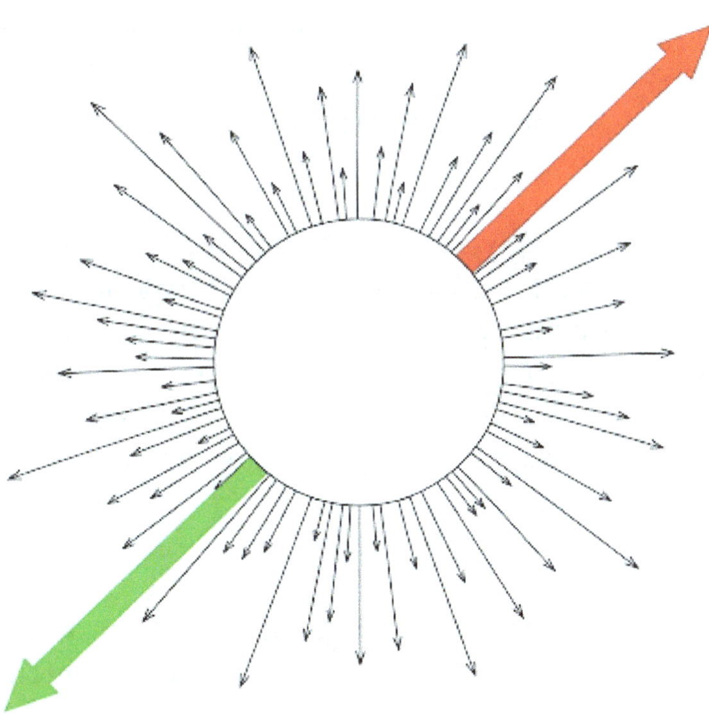

Figure 17.2: A visual representation of an Infinite
Array of Probabilities

To encourage a more favorable result, you should set an intention for what you want to happen. Once you've done that, let go of the need to control the outcome. Obsessing over possibilities can reinforce the very anxieties you're trying to avoid. Instead, visualize the successful outcome in detail, then release that thought and trust the process. Insisting on one particular outcome can blind you to even better possibilities you hadn't even considered. Instead of clinging to the need to control your fate, practice releasing the urge to have all the answers.

We can express this relationship mathematically through the **Trajectory Equation**. This equation shows how your beliefs and expectations can influence an outcome:

Trajectory (T) + Belief/ Expectation (B) → Influenced Outcome (O)

Where:
T = The current direction or momentum of your life or a situation.
B = Your emotional belief about what will happen.
O = An outcome increasingly likely to match your belief (though not guaranteed).

This equation doesn't promise results; it highlights your influence. The more consistently your belief aligns with your preferred direction, and excites feelings in you then the more your actions, attention, and decisions will support that path.

Bringing It All Together

The main takeaway is that at any given moment, unlimited potential outcomes exist as unlimited probabilities. Focusing exclusively on a single expected negative outcome can limit your perception and responsiveness to other, possibly more favorable, probabilities. By understanding and applying **Trajectory Shift principles**, we recognize that our beliefs can have a strong impact on how we view our reality and what's possible. When we consciously choose to shift our trajectory, we open ourselves to the full range of possibilities that exist in every moment.

Reflective question

What attachments to negative expectations am I ready to release, and what action can I take to let go and trust the process of a more favorable outcome unfolding?

Chapter Summary: This chapter introduces the Trajectory Equation for shifting outcomes by altering probabilities through expectations and beliefs. Negative expectations create resistance; reframing to optimistic, flexible narratives like "I remain open to the best outcome" dissolves barriers. Reinforce with intention-setting, visualization, and release of control, as per T + B → O. Conscious adjustments expand possibilities and invite supportive realities.

A Harvest of Trust

The world begins with held and shallow breath,
Where thorny dark vines weave fear and death.
Shadowed figures reach from cracked stone ground,
Grasping for a share that can't be found.
A single shriveled apple, prized yet small,
Provokes the fight, the hunger to take all.
This lens of scarcity, a ceaseless war,
Closes the door on all that could be more.
But look, where expectation starts to bend,
A glowing vortex marks the way to transcend.
The inner vision loosens its tight grip,
Allowing a new narrative to slip:
"I will remain open, though I cannot see,
And trust the outcome meant for me."
This softened turn, this quiet, fresh embrace,
Becomes the bridge where old constraints erase.
Beyond the portal, where the light descends,
A softer truth begins, and fear suspends.
A flourishing apple tree, majestic, tall,
Its laden boughs bear fruit enough for all.
Luminous gifts hang ready for the hand,
Abundant, ripe, in this vibrant land.
Here, figures walk with ease and steady peace,
Surrounded by the joy of wide release.
This shift from constriction to open air
Makes room for all we were born to share.
The course remains, the trajectory is set,
Yet what we expect defines what we get.
Release the grasping tether to the lack,
And watch the wealth come flowing back.
For harvest comes not by control's demand,
But by the trust that guides the arrow's hand.

Chapter XVIII: The Crucible Edge: The Forging Fire of Resilience

Figure 18.1: Forging Fire: Embracing the heat of transformation. This is what it feels like to turn adversity into empowerment.

The Crucible Edge:
Forging Fire, a term I created to describe a transformative experience, came when I discovered the power of the Energetic Resonance Effect. In that process, I found a new source of hope. By practicing these techniques, I moved forward, no longer letting past experiences dictate my future. Through transmuting resilience, pain shifted into empowerment.

A **Forging Fire Moment** is a transformative period when an individual overcomes overwhelming adversity and hopelessness by drawing on inner strength, choosing growth and renewal over being defined by struggle. It is the point when extreme hardship becomes a catalyst for resilience. Like metal in a furnace, crushing trials forge character, making it stronger and more enduring.

Reflective question - Have you experienced a Forging Fire Moment in your life?

Chapter Summary: This chapter introduces the Forging Fire Moment, a pivotal adversity sparking transformation, as the author experienced through discovering the Energetic Resonance Effect to heal wounds and reclaim agency. Resilience forges strength from struggle, like metal tempered in heat, turning pain into enduring hope and power. The lived transmutation process shifts pain to purpose.

The Forging Fire

The furnace claimed the life I knew,

A weight of flame that crushed me through,

Until the blaze remade the core,

A soul that burns yet aches no more.

Not merely mended from the scar,

But tempered bright through trials far;

The fire unbound what pain confined,

And forged its strength in heart and mind.

The past may whisper through the night,

Yet still I hold to its light;

The spark, by storm and strife, now rife,

Fuels the forge that shapes my life.

Figure 18.2: The **Chronos-Alchemica Engine,** A delicate brass instrument that distills the raw power of adversity into steady, enduring resilience.

Figure 18.2: The Chronos-Alchemica Engine, monument to applied metaphysics resembles a grand steampunk apparatus gleaming with brass, gears, and winding pipes, a Chronos-Alchemica Engine designed to process intangible concepts. Adversity, poured in via the burnished brass hopper, is subjected to immense pressure and heat within the labyrinthine network of valves and conduits. Its chaotic essence is drawn into the central containment vessel, where it is purified and stabilized by the shimmering green electrical arc of Intent. Gauges and dials meticulously track the conversion rate, ensuring that the volatile inputs are transformed rather than exploded. What drips into the collection vessels below is not the bitterness of the challenge, but the heavy, unshakable elixir of experience, a concentrated essence of Resilience.

Chapter XIX: The Prism Threshold: Advanced Energetic Influence

Figure 19.:1 A visual representation of **A Spectrum of Inner Change**.

Figure 19.1 This multi-layered conceptual diagram traces the flow from inner states to global interaction. At the top, it transitions from the brain (cognition) to the heart (emotion and well-being), progressing through abstract themes: connection and release, stability, direction, growth, perception and sight, clarity and illumination, and expression and identity (theatrical masks). Beneath, three focal areas emerge: digital communication and audio, upward progress and momentum, and self-reflection and awareness. These strands converge into interpersonal dialogue of shared energy, expanding outward to a globe encircled by radiating human figures.

The Multiple Dimensions of Transmutation

Transmutation is a process that unfolds across multiple levels of human experience, with each stage preparing the foundation for the next. At its most basic level, **beginners** develop greater ability to transmute their thoughts into felt sensations, bridging the gap between intellect and embodied experience. This step establishes the initial awareness that what you think and believe is not confined to your mind, but can be felt and processed physically in the body.

As the practice progresses, it enters the **intermediate** level. At this stage, the focus shifts to directly facing difficult emotions. Feelings like self-doubt, anxiety, or uncertainty are no longer avoided or dismissed. Instead, practitioners learn to stay present with these sensations, observing their texture and flow, until the energy within can be understood and gradually reshaped and transformed. This phase marks the beginning of true Elevated Energetic Transformation, where avoidance gives way to intentional engagement.

At the **advanced** level, transmutation expands beyond individual experience into the bioenergetic field of the environment itself. The practitioner learns to direct intention outward, creating a palpable influence on the energy of a room or group. This capacity extends from internal mastery into relational and collective dynamics. I call this skill **Energetic Influence,** a concept first introduced in Chapter 14, the deliberate projection of refined energy through the bioenergetic field, uplifting not only the self but also those within its reach.

Specialized Transmutational Pathways

Through dedicated practice, individuals often discover sensitivity or innate ability in transmuting specific patterns. These are what I refer to as **Transmutational Pathways**.

For example, the tense and restrictive nature of fear can be softened and expanded into a state of self assured resilience. The heavy weight of despair can be lightened into a renewed sense of hope and possibilities. The restless unease of self loathing and uncertainty can be shifted into inner knowing, and inner confidence that emerges from improved intuition. Likewise, the wounds of trauma may be reshaped into wisdom and resilience, offering both depth and strength. While a defensive posture of cynicism can be transformed into genuine optimism, while recurring patterns of self-doubt may give way to authentic self-expression and a greater sense of integrity.

These pathways show that transmutation is not a theoretical concept but an applied practice. Each shift alters both internal states and external behavior, producing lasting change through consistent practice and engagement.

Advanced Transmutational Methodologies

These sophisticated techniques emerge from consistent foundational work. They require both refined skill and the energetic capacity that develops over time.

I call the process of optimizing an already elevated feeling **Amplified Transmutation**. It is the practice of using concentrated focus and energetic finesse to take a beneficial feeling state that arises from the Energetic Resonance Effect, and refine it into its most potent form. The goal is to consciously strengthen the energy behind what is already present, making it more potent and powerful than before.

What this looks like in practice: imagine you are feeling uplifted and energized on a particular day. You then choose to elevate that state further through subtle focus on enhancing the sensation, encouraging and coaxing it along the feeling to expand and intensify it. This deliberate nurturing of an elevated state is Amplified Transmutation.

Foundational Practices for Energetic Capacity

To support and sustain this advanced work, focus on three key areas of energetic conservation:

1. **Minimize External Disruptions:** This does not mean avoiding conflict, but rather reducing unnecessary drama and friction in daily interactions. By fostering cohesion, you conserve energy and remain committed to transmuting your highest energetic expression forward.

2. **Monitor Internal Patterns:** Becoming aware of, and limiting, energetic drains such as excessive worry, fear, self-criticism, gossip, stress or reactive conflict is crucial for preserving your energetic reserves.

3. **Reduce Digital Overload:** Overstimulation often arises from overworking, overcommitting, or excessive screen time. Being mindful of input from phones, media, and constant distractions protects you from unnecessary energetic depletion.

Exponential Layering & Persona Preview

Another advanced methodology is what I call **Exponential Layering**. This is the cumulative growth that results when each act of transmutation builds upon the last, much like adding fuel to an ever-growing fire. Repetition and consistency are essential here, as each session compounds previous gains, leading to accelerated progress. This momentum-based process allows transformation to occur at a gradual increasing rate. In essence we are exponentially layering through transmutation the elevated and uplifting feelings onto themselves. This in turn causes even stronger elevations in ones energetic field.

Another practice I invite my readers to explore is what I call **the Persona Preview,** an experiment in trying on different energetic identities. By stepping into a new energy, we can observe how it feels and discover whether it aligns with our authentic persona. Much like trying on clothing in a store, some versions of yourself may feel authentic and empowering, while others may not fit quite right. Either way, the experience remains temporary and free of pressure. The Persona Preview encourages a sense of freedom and playfulness in self-discovery, allowing you to engage with new possibilities before fully inhabiting them.

Conclusion

Through consistent practice of transmutational pathways and advanced methodologies such as Amplified Transmutation, Exponential Layering, and the Persona Preview, practitioners gradually refine their energetic presence and influence. These practices strengthen and expand one's transmutational abilities. The journey begins with learning to translate thought into felt sensation and culminates in the ability to shape collective fields through Energetic Influence. In this way, personal transmutation becomes inseparable from the greater movement of the collective, an ever-evolving field of shared transformation and conscious potential.

~ Imagine how different the world would be if everyone practiced the Energetic Resonance Effect regularly.

Chapter Summary: This chapter depicts a journey from mind to heart, integrating intellect and emotion for self-discovery and connection. Transmutation elevates thoughts into higher frequencies via pathways like fear to acceptance, culminating in Energetic Broadcast. Advanced methods, Amplified Transmutation, Exponential Layering, and

Persona Preview, accelerate authenticity. Consistent practice refines individuals and uplifts the collective field.

Figure 19.2: The Trajectory Shift Portal - A luminous vortex portal, alive with the vibrant energy of transformation, beckons the viewer to embark on a journey of change.

The principles discussed, from bridging the inner states to projecting refined influence, are best understood not only as abstract methodologies but as an embodied, rhythmic process. The following, **The Transmutation Cipher,** map this multi-layered journey, distilling the flow of energetic capacity, the pathways of personal shift, and the cumulative power of advanced practice into a concise, evocative guide. It is the music of transmutation itself:

The Transmutation Cipher

This cipher describes the deliberate shift of consciousness from analytical thought to embodied feeling, charting the structural and energetic pathways required for powerful personal transformation.

The Trajectory Key

The code is not written on stone or sky,
It forms where the inner and outer self lie.-

The mind descends to heart's own base,
To ground within an open space.

The masks dissolve in clarity,
Revealing true identity.

First feel the thought, then face the sting;
Let the inner current swing.

From fear to bold, from wounds to wise,
We watch the hopeful spirit rise.

Amplify the higher state,
Layer growth and guard the gate.

Seal the leaks and slow the drain,
To break the cycle, change the plane.

From thought to feel, the circuit seals;
The outward influence reveals.

A vortex spins, the work is done:
The shift is made; the light is won.

Chapter XX: The Unbecoming: Alchemical Gold and Exponential Expansion

Figure 20.1: A visual representation of **The Unbecoming**

Figure 20.1: The Unbecoming: A journey from physical grounding to radiant consciousness, as the inner alchemist refines and expands the self, inspiring a new way of being.

The Unbecoming: Alchemical Gold and Exponential Expansion

Elevated Energetic Transformation is a powerful shift in how your mind operates, more than just acquiring new facts, it's a fundamental change in your awareness. As you become more mindful of your thoughts, you release old automatic habits and open yourself to experiencing the world anew. This process frees your mind, letting you move beyond the limits of ego and routine to access your fullest potential. The result is a flexible, creative mind that connects diverse ideas, ignites fresh inspiration, and sharpens intuition. This transformation isn't about being "smarter" in the usual way; it's about rediscovering your inner wisdom, enabling you to navigate life with greater intention and impact.

This expansion can be likened to the journey of alchemy, where a humble substance like mercury is carefully refined through heating and cleansing to become valuable gold. Similarly, your mind undergoes a purposeful process of transformation, requiring focused effort and appreciation for each stage. This is not an accidental change but a dedicated path toward elevated transformation and energetic renewal.

This transformation is a conscious and intentional journey that reshapes you into something completely new. Just like the alchemist, you can choose to go through this process, shaping a new way of existing and becoming so much more than you were before. The new "you" is like alchemical gold, pure and valuable, a shining example of the focused work you put in.

Just as the alchemist took gradual, focused steps to create something new, your personal transformation happens little by little. I think of this as engaging in your own renewal.

Purpose

By making space for the practice of the E.E.T., we are committing to our own improvement. This commitment involves shifting our inner energetic state through the techniques in this book. In doing so, we are communicating to the world, through our elevated energetic vibration, how we choose to exist in this lifetime.

To be the wellspring of your own energy is to awaken a self-sustaining source within, one that continuously fuels your growth, inspires your presence, and empowers you to transform from the inside out.

By embracing this practice, we can inspire others to join us in their own energetic shift. We don't have to convince them; we just need to let our actions speak for themselves through the tangible impact of our own transformation. After all, if change is to start anywhere, why not let it begin with each of us? Why not create a version of ourselves that embodies the change we want to see in the world?

The Inward Turn

As you begin to follow the steps for creating the E.E.T., you may find yourself drawn to spending part of your day in quiet reflection. The ways you once filled your free time may start to feel less satisfying.

As you evolve, you might come to value more time devoted to practicing this rewarding art. You may also find yourself growing more intentional with how you spend your free moments and the people you choose to share them with.

In this process of change, it feels as though the rhythm of the world has yet to fully find its beat alongside mine, as if we are still moving to slightly different tempos, quietly out of sync in this unfolding dance through time.

Your Expansion

As we diligently practice the techniques of the E.R.E., powerful shifts begin to arise within us, emerging effortlessly from our committed effort. Our energetic influence expands exponentially, yet this growth requires conscious and consistent practice.

Our existence blends the physical and the energetic, entwined realities that shape our experience. The energetic realm connects to the soul's journey, while the physical grounds us in tangible life. By Gradually refining our energetic blueprint, we transform our perspective, reshaping how we see ourselves and how we manifest physically. Small adjustments expand outward like echoes in a chamber, igniting transformation throughout our environment.

The Universal Harmonic of Exponential Expansion

Exponential Expansion is not random; it follows a precise, elegant pattern of growth that appears throughout creation itself. To grasp the true magnitude of this change, we look to the cosmos.

The Golden Ratio ϕ, often called "the Divine Proportion", is a universal constant of harmonious, accelerating growth, functioning like a core frequency of creation.

The image of a "radiant column of golden energy spiraling upward" exponentially describes a phenomenon modeled by the Golden Spiral. This spiral, geometrically defined by ϕ, reveals a form of expansion that grows ever larger while remaining true to its original pattern.

Aligning E.E.T. with this principle means your personal transformation is not just a human effort, but an act of synchronization with the fundamental pulse of the universe. Your journey from trauma to purpose follows the most elegant and efficient blueprint for growth available, affirming that your newly refined self, the "alchemical gold", is stabilizing into a state of coherent, self-sustaining wholeness.

Reflective question
After reading about these concepts, which of your "dormant powers" are you ready to activate, and what would that look like in your life?

~ Nurture curiosity, look beyond familiar ideas, question convention, and shape your own path to understanding.

Chapter summary: This chapter synthesizes the core principles of E.E.T., moving beyond the initial introduction toward full integration, a stage that elevates awareness beyond ego limitations and restores connection with inner wisdom for intentional, conscious living. Using the metaphor of personal alchemy, it emphasizes that transformation unfolds through sustained effort, culminating in a renewed self whose natural energetic presence, not persuasion, inspires others. This integration deepens through a final exploration of The Inward Turn, refining your intentional use of time and relationships. The journey culminates in Expansion, where your evolving presence generates transformative ripples across all aspects of life exponentially expanding, completing the path toward powerful, whole-being change and a reawakened perception of the world.

This internal transformation unfolds not only in thought but also in feeling. The poem that follows reflects the soulful experience of becoming the alchemist of one's own being.

The Inner Alchemist

A stagnant weight, entwined in time,
pulls me down through tangled vines.
Yet energies fuse and rise,
unfolding like the incoming tide,
transforming despair
into hope's warm embrace.
My being stirs, fully awake,
speaking truths beyond all words.
Gratitude blooms, shining bright,
sustained by the endless stream
of living light.

Chapter XXI: Language of the Measured Heart: Your Most Powerful Gift

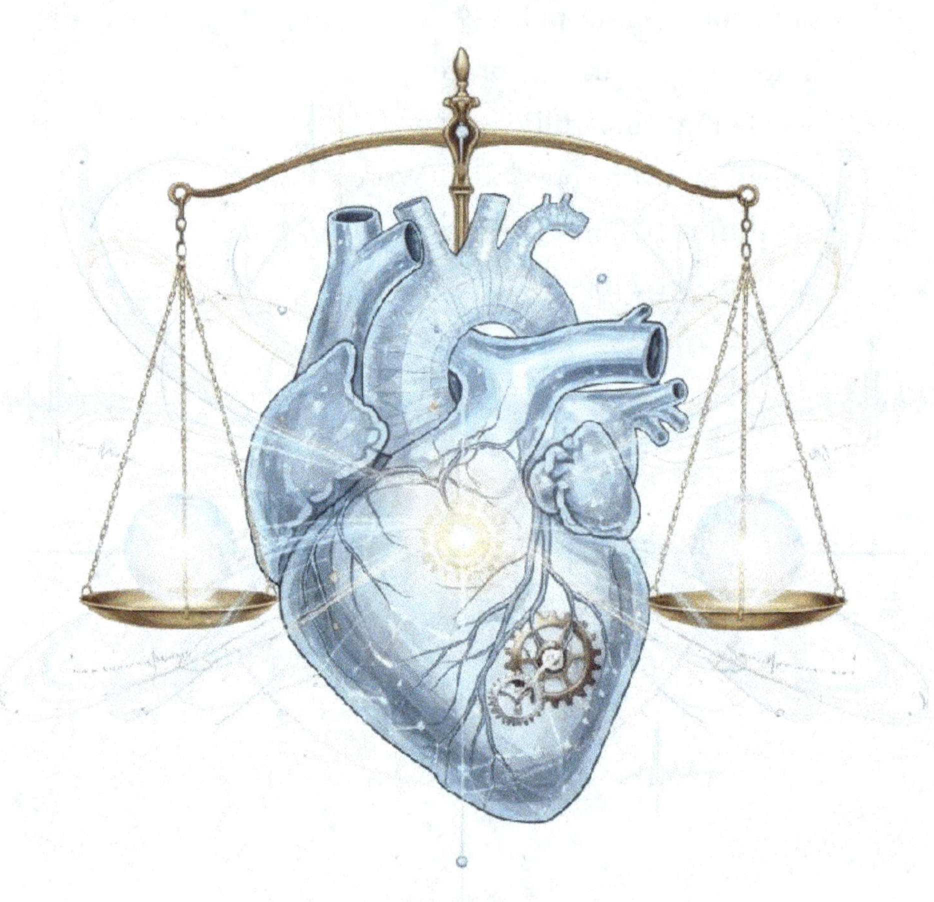

Figure 21.1: The Measured Heart: a crucible of balance, wisdom, and transformation.

Language of the measured heart

Years ago, after completing several immersive meditation sessions, I began receiving vivid visions of a large, regal, king-like presence. He appeared floating above me as a large, commanding figure draped in gold, his face striking with a bird's beak. Seated upon an immense stone throne with wide armrests, he radiated an intense aura of strength and authority. He exuded power and his deep, resonant laughter echoed through me. His energy was both intimidating, powerful and potent.

Curious, I asked during a meditation who he was. The answer I recieved: "Thoth" was his name. At the time, I had never heard this name, nor was I familiar with the mythology attached to it. Several years later, I came across an online post describing a nearly identical figure. The descriptions and images matched my visions perfectly, and he was also named Thoth. The recognition stunned me. I realized that in those meditations, I had connected with a presence I had never consciously encountered.

The Wisdom of a God

Further research revealed that Thoth was among the most significant deities in Egyptian religion, the god of magic, writing, sacred texts, mathematics, science, and wisdom. Patron of scribes and master of knowledge, he is often depicted with the head of the ibis, a bird revered in Egypt as a symbol of sacred intelligence.

I was struck by how Thoth's domains mirrored the very themes I had been exploring in this work. Inspiration for the book's direction began arriving with unusual frequency and clarity, as if something beyond myself were guiding the process. The connections felt unquestionable, as though the knowledge flowing through me was a modern reflection of the principles Thoth embodies.

~ Unconditional self-love makes you unstoppable in becoming your greatest version.

Chapter Summary: *Connecting Ancient Wisdom to Modern Transformation*

The author's unexpected connection to Thoth, the Egyptian god of magic, wisdom, and writing, forms a foundation for this book. Research revealed a parallel between his ancient legacy and the themes interwoven throughout these pages. Over time, the author came to see this work not merely as a personal project but as a living vessel for timeless wisdom, carrying forward the transformative essence embodied by Thoth. This book serves as a present-day transcription of principles for Elevated Energetic Transformation, inspired by the ancient teachings on consciousness and creation that Thoth represents.

Figure 21.2: Thoth, Lord of Ma'at and Wisdom: - The ancient Egyptian deity of wisdom and magic, seated regally on a grand stone throne.

Your Most Powerful Gift

You are a powerful creator. Your ability to effect meaningful change lies in where you place your energy. Though it may rest dormant, it awakens with small shifts that lead to far greater transformations. As you develop this skill, you begin shaping a more intentional reality. I hope this book encourages you to embrace your most authentic self. Authenticity is a rare gift in a world of imitation. It is the foundation of your integrity and cannot be taken from you. By choosing your true self, you claim a radical freedom in a culture that urges strict conformity.

As you practice the Energetic Resonance Effect, others may notice subtle changes in you. They might look at you with curiosity, sensing something they cannot yet identify. Take this as confirmation that your energy has begun to shift. You have crossed a threshold, becoming a more authentic, magnetic version of yourself.

With continued practice, you refine this transformation. You grow confident in your ability to transmute your energy and discover a path where there is everything to gain and nothing to lose. With steady, minimal effort, you elevate self-confidence, expand magnetism, and cultivate a clearer, more empowered presence.

Even if you choose not to practice this process, remember: your energy is always communicating with the world. By recognizing this, you can walk with greater mindfulness and purpose. Living in authenticity is your birth right and should always be encouraged within.

It is my hope that this book inspires a movement toward the ongoing practice of E.E.T. and the E.R.E and A.M.E, guiding you into a more authentic and intentional way of existing. Here lies your chance to draw from an endless well of empowering energy, creating shifts that build upon themselves.

~ A day spent practicing the Energetic Resonance Effect is a day we choose to live in our truest state.

The Oblique Origin

We did not arrive broken
only retuned
for a different sun.

What they call sensitivity
is a finer antenna,
listening to the Great Field's whisper
an array translating
the oceanic frequencies of being.

Our minds, inverse engines,
thrive on oblique calculus
fractals within fractals,
where others draw straight lines.

We chart unseen dimensions,
hybrid maps wrought from
starlight memory
and patient clay.

This is the upgrade:
friction transmuted
into kinetic light,
feeling the world so sharply
the soul must widen its shell.

We carry new code,
a collective leap through
magnetic currents,
drawing the future near.

Not strangers here,
but a conscious lineage
recalibrating its engines.

And in this final fire,
the path unfolds
boundless awareness,
alive in the hyper-attuned,
the intricate mind,
the beautifully oblique strain.

A Final Note

This path is more than just a framework, it is an accessible activation for everyone. Rooted in the lived reality of neurodivergence, it invites all to develop fluency in managing their own energy. As clarity grows within you, you begin to effortlessly sense the energetic fields of others, gaining a deep intuitive insight to perceive true intentions beyond words and actions. You carry within you a trusted internal compass to navigate the energetic terrain of life. Embrace that your sensitivity is a rare strength, your differences are a deliberate design, and your power lies in transforming challenges into a magnetic force. Move forward with confidence in the wisdom of your inverse engine, consciously shaping the limitless reality meant for you. The world awaits the frequency of your genuine self, this message transcends neurodivergence to inspire universal awakening.

Figure 21.4: Cosmic Rebirth marks having shed layers to reveal inner brilliance, signifying a shimmering gateway to the next evolution. The universe of possibility awaits as the journey begins again: bolder, brighter, and infinitely you

~ Refuse the expected course laid before you, be the rare spark, the anomaly. Seek the hidden passage, and let your difference illuminate your own way.

A Message of Hope and Transformation

The Journey of E.E.T.: From the roots of your being to the light of self-acceptance, your unique path is one of hope, peace, and renewal. Embrace your brilliance and step into your truest self.

This book is for anyone ready to move beyond mere survival and step into a journey of growth and transformation. It has been my sincere hope to offer encouragement and a new path forward to those wrestling with despair. Through the concepts shared here, including E.E.T., I aim to have guided you toward a more hopeful and empowered future.

I also want this book to speak directly to the many who navigate the world with neurodivergent traits. I recognize the real struggles and deep feelings of isolation that you many of you face. This work is meant to bring you relief and validation, equipping you with fresh tools and perspectives to approach life with greater confidence.

Ultimately, this book stands as a testament to the belief that change is within reach. Whether you identify as neurodivergent, are a trauma survivor, struggle with depression, or find yourself feeling stuck in life, I hope you have found solace and strength within these pages. Remember, your journey is uniquely yours, and with the right knowledge and support, you have the power to transform your life and embrace peace in your authentic self. Transformation begins with the choice to embark on it, today.

~ Fret less, transmute more.

Ready to shift further...?

A f t e r w o r d :

Thank you for joining me on this journey. My hope is that the concepts and practices shared within these pages have opened your mind to new possibilities and empowered you to take the first steps on your own path to energetic transformation.

This book represents the culmination of years of study, practice, and personal discovery. My intention was to create a guide that is both accessible and insightful, helping you understand the subtle forces that shape our lives and providing the tools to work with them consciously.

The journey to Elevated Energetic Transformation is not a final destination but a continuous process of learning and growth. The insights you've gained here are just the beginning. I believe true transformation unfolds in community and through direct, guided experience.

For those ready to dive deeper and accelerate their practice, I invite you to join one of my live in person sessions or master classes. These sessions offer a supportive environment for hands-on practice, personalized guidance, and the opportunity to connect with a community of like minded, fellow seekers.

Find my books in paperback and ebook wherever you choose to shop.
I'm excited to connect with you there and warmly invite you to reach out with any questions or thoughts at: AlchemicalGoldPublishing@gmail.com.

Thank you again for your trust and for embarking on this powerful journey. I look forward to supporting you on your path.

With gratitude,

Greg Hollis

About the Author

Greg Hollis is the author of this work, which represents a three-year intensive project distilling his unique methodology into a practical guide. As the founder and principal catalyst behind his Neuro-inverse approach, he specializes in Elevated Energetic Transformation, a process shaped by his own journey of healing and growth. Greg draws on eight years of experience in the healing arts, which laid the foundation for his insights.

Alphabetical Index & Definitions:

The following glossary serves as a reference for the specialized terminology and frameworks utilized within this work. To gain a full understanding of the Elevated Energetic Transformation process, it is helpful to have a clear grasp of these core concepts. Refer to these definitions as you progress through the chapters to ensure a consistent understanding of the energetic principles and exercises presented.

1. **Alchemical Gold:** The fragments left behind by a dismantled Box or old identity. It represents the valuable energy released through transmutation and the breaking of societal structures.

2. **Amplified Transmutation:** The culmination of an energetic process, representing the peak and most expansive state an energy can reach.

3. **Anchor Exercise:** A grounding technique that uses visualization and breath to relax the mind during stress. It shifts focus from racing thoughts to physical sensations to help release tension and an overactive mind.

4. **Authentic Magnetic Essence (A.M.E.):** The transmutation of one's embodied sensual energy into magnetic attraction, cultivating a presence that draws others in. This process functions as a subset of the Energetic Resonance Effect.

5. **Authenticity:** The expression of one's truest self, projected outward without self-judgment or pretense.

6. **B.E.T.E.R. Framework (The):** A five-step process for creating the Energetic Resonance Effect. The acronym stands for: Be, Elevate, Transmute, Excite and Amplify, and Radiate and Repeat.

7. **Core Energetic Signature:** The core frequency an individual projects, maintains, and inevitably gravitates toward emitting.

8. **Dormant Power:** The passive hesitation or refusal to take inspired action toward something we truly want. This inaction often stems from fear, complacency, or loss of belief in our ability to succeed in that particular area.

9. **Elevated Energetic Transformation (E.E.T.):** The proprietary, accelerated, and systematic methodology that moves beyond basic energetic awareness. E.E.T. specifically targets the source energetic frequency to trigger irreversible and authentic shifts across all domains of life, culminating in a state of sustained elevated being.

10. **Energetic Anchor Effect (E.A.E.) (The):** Describes how a practitioner, through the Energetic Resonance Equation (E.R.E.), becomes the stabilizing frequency of their environment. When you are present, energy flows easily, harmony increases, and those around you feel uplifted. When you are absent, the environment's baseline frequency returns, often leading to stagnation or decline. The E.A.E. reveals that conscious presence sustains coherence within any shared energetic field.

11. **Energetic Autopilot:** A sustained state of the Energetic Resonance Effect that operates without continuous active focus.

12. **Energetic Congruence:** A state where actions, words, and decisions reflect your inner energy: your Authentic Magnetic Essence (A.M.E.). In this state, your expression and intention merge into a unified signal, allowing the Energetic Resonance Effect (E.R.E) to unfold with ease.

13. **Energetic Derailment:** A high-resistance state that occurs when someone tries to force a rapid emotional or energetic shift while already in strong momentum: such as significant overwhelm or emotional flooding. The remedy is to distract the mind, allowing momentum to slow before making a balanced, intentional shift.

14. **Energetic Detachment:** Describes someone who appears emotionally muted and closed-off, often harboring simmering anger beneath the surface. This hidden tension erodes optimism by fostering negativity, withdrawal, and a sense of powerless disconnection from positive possibilities.

15. **Energetic Fear Regulation:** The intentional practice of transforming a negative feeling, emotion, or thought into a positive, higher-vibrational one. It is the process of consciously changing your internal energy from a dense, lower frequency to a lighter, more elevated state.

16. **Energetic Feedback Loop:** A process of linking our energy back into itself.

17. **Energetic Incongruence:** A state of dissonance that occurs when fear, doubt, or external conditioning distort your A.M.E. This misalignment weakens your energetic transmission, causing disruptions in the flow of Authentic Magnetism (A.M.) and reducing the potency of your presence.

18. **Energetic Influence:** The capacity of a single individual, through conscious intention and the practice of Energetic Coherence & Expansion (E.R.E.), to positively affect and guide the collective bioenergetic field or atmosphere of a group, leading to transformative shifts within the shared energetic experience.

19. **Energetic Interference:** The disruption of your inner, balanced energetic state. It is the static or noise created by negative thoughts or outside events that can knock your energy off course.

20. **Energetic Magic (a.k.a. Energetic Transmutation):** Creating real change at your core, not just shifting surface habits, but transforming your inner foundation. It is a powerful shift achieved by altering your energetic state through the conversion of thought into felt experience, fundamentally changing your identity from the inside out.

21. **Energetic Magnetization:** The intentional practice of recharging your personal energy, which in turn strengthens your internal magnetism. This process enables you to draw in people, circumstances, and opportunities that match the energy you're radiating.

22. **Energetic Misinterpretation:** When others mistakenly interpret your self-directed energy as social attention or interest, causing unintended misunderstandings or discomfort.

23. **Energetic Resonance Effect:** The intentional and gracious practice of cultivating a harmonious inner state that infuses the shared field with coherent, uplifting energy. Through this attuned presence, a subtle nonverbal resonance emerges, an exchange that transcends words and improves mutual connection.

24. **Energetic Slop:** Habitual mismanagement of energy through inefficient, unproductive, and draining expenditure. Over time, this creates depleted reserves, scattered focus, and ultimately dissatisfaction and restlessness.

25. **Energetic Transformation:** The base term for the fundamental, conscious process of recognizing, defining, and intentionally regulating one's subtle energy states, including emotional, mental, and vibrational frequencies, to induce desired change. It is a process of personal transmutation that creates real change at your core.

26. **Energetic Waves:** The invisible waves of uplifting energy that emanate from a practitioner, creating sympathetic frequencies that enhance both the individual and those within their energetic field.

27. **Enhanced Frisson Effect (The):** An amplified physiological and emotional response, characterized by a powerful, whole-body sensation of excitement and potency, often accompanied by tingling, chills, or euphoria. This phenomenon arises when the Energetic Resonance Effect is integrated with and transmutes the traditional frisson response, resulting in a significantly heightened experience of inner radiance and transformation.

28. **Entrenched Beliefs:** Psychological barriers that form when outdated self-perceptions become so fixed they limit our efforts, constrain achievement, and prevent us from recognizing our current potential.

29. **Exponential Layering:** An act of transmuting uplifting energy that continuously layers onto itself, resulting in exponential growth. By continuously building upon it, like feeding a fire, we nurture its growth and expansion.

30. **Extraordinary Energetic Potentials:** A collection of five Extraordinary Energetic Potentials (Optimism, Transmutation, Imagination, Resilience, and Authenticity) that are

often overlooked but inherently available to all of us. By becoming consciously aware of these abilities, we can unlock their transformative potential in our daily lives.

31. **Exuberant:** Filled with or characterized by a lively energy and excitement.

32. **Fear Bound:** A person who is unconsciously addicted to allowing fear to influence their important decisions. This fear-based response clouds their judgment, often resulting in mediocre or suboptimal outcomes.

33. **Focused Energy Shaping:** The practice of intentionally directing your energy with awareness of how your hormonal state influences it. Instead of suppressing impulses, you refine and balance your internal energy flow, honoring instinctive signals while choosing a steady frequency that guides your thoughts, emotions, body, hormones, and interactions.

34. **Forging Fire Moment:** A transformative period where an individual overcomes overwhelming adversity and hopelessness by drawing on inner resilience, choosing growth and renewal over being defined by past struggles. This is the point when extreme adversity becomes a catalyst for resilience.

35. **Frequency:** The quality of the wave that energy embodies. This determines the inherent characteristic of the energy: for example, joy has a higher frequency than sadness.

36. **Frequency Mixing:** An advanced technique of mixing multiple uplifting and complementary frequencies together to create a more powerful combined effect.

37. **Imposter Syndrome:** The persistent inability to believe that one's success is deserved or has been legitimately achieved as a result of one's own efforts or skills.

38. **Inner Catalyst:** The subtle yet pleasant vibration you feel in your chest. It is the internal sensation that acts as a starting point, or ignition point, for your energetic work.

39. **Intentional Presence:** A form of non-verbal communication where your active engagement and mindful quietness become the message. It is a deliberate choice to use your quiet presence to connect with others on a greater, more sincere level.

40. **Inverse Engine (The):** The conceptual and active process of Post-Traumatic Transmutation, converting the potent psychological energy of early adversity and unmet validation into a powerful, sustainable fuel for high achievement and deliberate personal growth.

41. **Masking:** The conscious or unconscious act of hiding neurodivergent traits to fit social norms, often by suppressing behaviors and mimicking typical social cues. It serves as a coping mechanism but can lead to stress and loss of authenticity, commonly experienced by neurodivergent individuals.

42. **Malleable Mind:** The brain's natural ability to adapt, reorganize, and reshape itself in response to experience, environment, and internal change. In the context of

neurodivergence and trauma, it reflects the capacity to move beyond rigid, shame-based patterns into a more flexible and responsive way of being. At its core, it is what allows "Internal Weather" to shift from friction into growth..

43. **Metacognition:** The awareness and regulation of one's own thinking and learning processes, including planning, monitoring, and evaluating how to approach tasks. It involves thinking about thinking and is often linked with neurodivergent traits, where individuals may have unique ways of understanding and controlling their cognition.

44. **Negativity Loop:** A self-perpetuating, downward spiral of negative thoughts and emotions. It is a destructive cycle where dwelling on problems fuels feelings of despair, shame, and hopelessness, making it feel impossible to escape.

45. **Neuro-inverse:** Reframes neurodivergence not as a biological error, but as a deliberate cognitive upgrade. It positions the neurodivergent brain as an architecture designed for high-order specialization, replacing standard processing pathways with systems capable of deep pattern synthesis, sustained hyper-focus, and divergent innovation. Within this model, what is commonly labeled as "disorder" becomes the inherent friction of a high-performance system operating beyond conventional cognitive constraints.

46. **Neurodivergent Hyper-focus Fatigue (a.k.a. neurodivergent burnout):** A term for the intense physical and mental exhaustion that follows a prolonged period of intense focus, where a person becomes so engrossed in a task that they neglect their own basic needs.

47. **Optimism:** A forward-looking mindset that sees possibilities and expects a favorable outcome, regardless of external circumstances.

48. **Persona Preview (The):** This focuses on the process of testing whether a frequency and the emerging identity match, emphasizing resonance and authenticity.

49. **Phase:** The state of coherence or synchronization between your thought and your feeling. Achieving this state is essential for effective energetic transformation.

50. **Principle Catalyst:** The moment we stop fighting the weather of our minds and start giving our specific processors the fuel they require. It is the bridge between surviving a traumatic past and thriving in a calibrated present.

51. **Prismatic Core:** The pure, high-vibrational energetic center of the transformed self. It is the authentic, radiant identity, the alchemical gold, that is refined and extracted through the intense, alchemical fusion of opposing low-vibrational forces, like pain and shame, and the conscious will.

52. **PTGI:** Refers to either a psychological assessment tool or a rendering method used in Minecraft. In psychology, it stands for the Post-Traumatic Growth Inventory, a 21-item questionnaire designed to measure positive personal changes following trauma. It assesses areas such as strengthened relationships, new possibilities, increased personal strength, and a fuller appreciation of life.

53. **Reciprocity Deficit (The):** Refers to the emotional and energetic toll that arises when authentic presence is continually sought and absorbed by others without conscious, mutual exchange. This one-sided pattern creates an unsustainable imbalance.

54. **Reflective Confidence:** Occurs when someone's genuine self-assurance unintentionally triggers insecurity in another person by serving as a mirror for their own self-doubt.

55. **Self-Honor Principle (The):** The transformative realization that self-compassion is the most crucial act for our well-being. This understanding that only we can care for ourselves allows us to build a foundation of self-respect and stop the cycle of self-rejection.

56. **Superimposition Principle (The):** Posits that the Energetic Resonance Effect occurs when a higher vibrational energy is intentionally superimposed onto a lower one. This process neutralizes the lower vibration, resulting in a transformative shift.

57. **Theta Wave Transmutational Imagination:** A focused state where theta brainwaves (3.5 to 7.5 Hz) link conscious thought with the subconscious, enabling intense creative visualization and intuitive insight. This state supports transforming limiting beliefs and mental patterns into new possibilities by reshaping mental blueprints with clarity and potential.

58. **Thoth, Lord of Ma'at and Wisdom:** In ancient Egyptian mythology, he is the deity of the moon, writing, magic, and the measurement of time. He is acknowledged as a foundational spiritual source of the energetic principles and guidance related to transformation and heart-centered awareness.

59. **Trajectory Equation:** Expresses how your current life direction or situation Trajectory, (T), combined with your beliefs and expectations (B), interact to influence the likelihood of a resulting outcome (O). This model shows that while outcomes are not guaranteed, your mindset plays a crucial role in shaping what becomes more probable.

60. **Transducer / Feeler:** A person who perceives and interprets subtle energies and vibrations through the sense of feeling, experiencing intuitive impressions somatically via bodily sensations, emotional resonance, and energetic shifts.

61. **Transmutation:** The art of transforming one substance, form, or state into another. In this book, it refers to the process through which thoughts crystallize into feelings, the fundamental method for creating change at the level of identity.

62. **Transmutational Pathways:** Specific, practiced abilities that transform challenging inner states, such as fear or despair, into elevated ones, such as calm resilience or hope, making the process of transmutation tangible and resulting in lasting positive change.

63. **Tree Networking:** An active effort to reconnect with nature's supportive energies through conscious communion with trees.

64. **Unintended Life (The):** A life lived on autopilot, where an individual drifts without conscious purpose. It is an existence defined by passivity rather than intention, as a person reacts to external circumstances and societal expectations instead of making deliberate choices. This leads to a feeling of aimlessness and disconnection from one's true potential.

65. **Uniqueness Trap (The):** The unconscious belief that your suffering is uniquely special, which creates a false sense of uniqueness that blocks compassion, connection, and ultimately, your capacity for healing.

66. **Vibrational Coaxing:** The active process of using focused attention to amplify and sustain a subtle energetic state within the body.

67. **Viral Limitations:** The phenomenon where a person's limiting beliefs or negative perspectives are voiced and then unknowingly adopted by others. This creates a shared and destructive worldview, reinforcing the limitations and making them more difficult for everyone to overcome.

68. **Word Transference:** The process by which our spoken words carry energy that shapes our internal state and external reality. What we consistently say about ourselves and our circumstances becomes absorbed by our body and mind, causing us to embody those characteristics and attract corresponding outcomes.

Intellectual Influences:

Bustamante, A. (n.d.). Everyday Spy Podcast [YouTube channel]. YouTube. https://www.youtube.com/@EverydaySpyPodcast

Bustamante, A. (YYYY, Month Day). Video title in sentence case [Video]. YouTube. https://youtube.com/shorts/_HKajWyAq_M

Carhart-Harris, R. L., Erritzoe, D., Williams, T., Stone, J. M., Evans, J., Turkheimer, A., Spiegelberg, T., & Nutt, D. J. (2012). Neural correlates of the psychedelic state as determined by fMRI studies with psilocybin. Proceedings of the National Academy of Sciences, 109(6), 2138–2143. https://doi.org/10.1073/pnas.1119598109

Colver, M. C., & El-Alayli, A. (2016). Getting aesthetic chills from music: The connection between openness to experience and frisson. Psychology of Music, 44(6), 1400–1412. https://doi.org/10.1177/0305735615622051

Davies, J. (n.d.). How theta waves boost your intuition & creativity and how to generate them. Learning Mind. https://www.learning-mind.com/theta-waves/

Fraser, W. (2024, October 28). Building trust & navigating conflict. Washington State Results Office. https://results.wa.gov/sites/default/files/WendyFraser_Oct28_HANDOUT.pdf

Gálvez, V., Watkins, A., & Glue, P. (2021). Safety and efficacy of psychedelic-assisted psychotherapy: A narrative review of current evidence and clinical considerations. Therapeutic Advances in Psychopharmacology, 11. https://doi.org/10.1177/20451253211029221

Grosz, D. E., Plioplys, S., Obeidallah, E. M., & Kuperman, G. (2021). Headaches in children with autism spectrum disorder: A systematic review and meta-analysis. Journal of Child Neurology, 36(7), 577–585. https://doi.org/10.1177/0883073820980590

Irau, C. [@carolina.irau]. (2024, January 7). Post describing the 'Marilyn Monroe effect' in an elderly relative [TikTok video]. TikTok. https://www.tiktok.com/t/ZP8JN9uQJ

Johnson, M. W., Griffiths, R. R., Hendricks, P. S., & Henningfield, J. E. (2018). The abuse potential of medical psilocybin according to the 8 factors of the Controlled Substances Act. Neuropharmacology, 142, 143–166. https://doi.org/10.1016/j.neuropharm.2018.05.012

Kurtzman, L. (2022, April 7). Psilocybin rewires the brain for people with depression: Study suggests new mechanism for how psychedelics affect the brain. University of California, San Francisco. https://www.ucsf.edu/news/2022/04/422606/psilocybin-rewires-brain-people-depression

Miles, A. [@chorusforlife]. (2024, August 31). Content description (up to 20 words) [TikTok video]. TikTok. https://www.tiktok.com/t/ZP8Up6avL/

Miller, S. K. (2022, December 20). Research shows neurodivergent individuals excel creatively. Psychology Today. https://www.psychologytoday.com/us/blog/eating-disorders-among-gender-expansive-and-neurodivergent-individuals/202212/research-shows

Nusbaum, E. C., & Silvia, P. J. (2011). Shivers and timbres: Personality and the experience of chills from music. Social Psychological and Personality Science, 2(6), 600–606. https://doi.org/10.1177/1948550611400216

Ott, T. (2020, September 9). Marilyn Monroe's relationship with her mother. Biography. https://www.biography.com/actors/marilyn-monroe-mother-relationship

Reiff, C. M., Richter, J. S., Sheman, K. L., & Nemeroff, C. B. (2020). Psychedelics and psychedelic-assisted psychotherapy. American Journal of Psychiatry, 177(5), 391–410. https://doi.org/10.1176/appi.ajp.2019.19010059

Sachs, M. E., Ellis, R. J., Schlaug, G., & Loui, P. (2016). Brain connectivity reflects human aesthetic responses to music. Social Cognitive and Affective Neuroscience, 11(11), 1718–1727. https://doi.org/10.1093/scan/nsw085

Studerus, E., Kometer, M., Hasler, F., & Vollenweider, F. X. (2011). Acute, subacute and long-term subjective effects of psilocybin in healthy humans: A pooled analysis of experimental studies. Journal of Psychopharmacology, 25(11), 1434–1452. https://doi.org/10.1177/0269881110382466

Tedeschi, R. G., & Calhoun, L. G. (1996). The posttraumatic growth inventory: Measuring the positive legacy of trauma. Journal of Traumatic Stress, 9(3), 455–471. https://doi.org/10.1002/jts.2490090305

Watts, R., & Luoma, J. B. (2020). The use of the psychological flexibility model to support psychedelic assisted therapy. Journal of Contextual Behavioral Science, 18, 64–72. https://doi.org/10.1016/j.jcbs.2020.08.002

Weinstein, E. (2019, September 2). The Marilyn Monroe effect: The nonverbal communication of confidence. Psych Central. psychcentral.com/blog/the-marilyn-monroe-effect-the-nonverbal-communication-of-confidence#1

Colophon:

This work represents a three-year intensive project meticulously crafted during the fall of 2025 in Denver, Colorado, USA

The text is set in Palatino at 12pt, chosen for its readability and contemporary feel. The display typeface used for chapters is also Palatino at 24pt, providing a bold complement to the main text. Quotes are set in Palatino at 12pt and rendered in bold italic. Poems are set in Palatino at 12pt.

The design and layout of this project were created using Apple Pages.

This project was printed on Glossy Coated Stock.

Special Thanks
I am grateful for the guidance of **Thoth**, which made this project possible.

- Created by Greg Hollis
- Publisher: Alchemical Gold
- Contact: AlchemicalGoldPublishing@gmail.com
- Available wherever books are sold.

Personal Notes: